W9-BBP-218

Withdrawn

MAY 0 5 2022

Northville District Library
212 West Cady St.
Northville, MI 48167

The [...] Public Library
[...] Street
[...]

PRAISE FOR GABRIELLE BERNSTEIN
AND *HAPPY DAYS*

*"This book is a game-changer filled with honesty and openne[.]
The vulnerability Gabby offers within the pages of* Happy Da[.]
*will make you feel less alone. And, perhaps, willing to face
some of your own fears with an open heart."*

– Dr. Shefali, *New York Times* best-selling author
and clinical psychologist

*"An act of extreme courage. . . . My hope is that this book
inspires the spiritual world."*

– Richard C. Schwartz, Ph.D., founder of
Internal Family Systems

"Gabrielle is the real thing. I respect her work immensely."
— Dr. Wayne Dyer

"A new role model."
— The New York Times

*Named "a new thought leader"
by Oprah's* Super Soul Sunday

HAPPY DAYS

ALSO BY
GABRIELLE BERNSTEIN

Books

Super Attractor*

Judgment Detox

The Universe Has Your Back*

Miracles Now*

May Cause Miracles

Spirit Junkie

Add More ~ing to Your Life

You Are the Guru

Cards

Super Attractor: A 52-Card Deck*

The Universe Has Your Back: A 52-Card Deck*

Miracles Now: A 62-Card Deck*

*Available from Hay House

Please visit:

Hay House USA: www.hayhouse.com®
Hay House Australia: www.hayhouse.com.au
Hay House UK: www.hayhouse.co.uk
Hay House India: www.hayhouse.co.in

***

HAPPY DAYS

The Guided Path from Trauma to Profound Freedom and Inner Peace

GABRIELLE BERNSTEIN

HAY HOUSE, INC.
Carlsbad, California • New York City
London • Sydney • New Delhi

Copyright © 2022 by Gabrielle Bernstein

Published in the United States by: Hay House, Inc.: www.hayhouse.com®
Published in Australia by: Hay House Australia Pty. Ltd.: www.hayhouse.com.au
Published in the United Kingdom by: Hay House UK, Ltd.: www.hayhouse.co.uk
Published in India by: Hay House Publishers India: www.hayhouse.co.in

Cover design: Tracey Edelstein
Interior design: Julie Davison
Indexer: J S Editorial, LLC

The cover of *No Bad Parts: Healing Trauma & Restoring Wholeness with the Internal Family Systems Model* by Richard C. Schwartz, Ph.D., on page 188 is reprinted by permission of Sounds True.

All rights reserved. No part of this book may be reproduced by any mechanical, photographic, or electronic process, or in the form of a phonographic recording; nor may it be stored in a retrieval system, transmitted, or otherwise be copied for public or private use—other than for "fair use" as brief quotations embodied in articles and reviews—without prior written permission of the publisher.

The author of this book does not dispense medical advice or prescribe the use of any technique as a form of treatment for physical, emotional, or medical problems without the advice of a physician, either directly or indirectly. The intent of the author is only to offer information of a general nature to help you in your quest for emotional, physical, and spiritual well-being. In the event you use any of the information in this book for yourself, the author and the publisher assume no responsibility for your actions.

Cataloging-in-Publication Data is on file at the Library of Congress

Hardcover ISBN: 978-1-4019-6549-5
Autographed Edition ISBN: 978-1-4019-6918-9
E-book ISBN: 978-1-4019-6550-1

10 9 8 7 6 5 4 3 2 1
1st edition, February 2022

Printed in the United States of America

For my husband, Zach.
Thank you for loving all of my
parts and helping me feel safer
than I ever thought possible.

CONTENTS

Foreword   xi

Acknowledgments   xv

Introduction: The Truth about This Book   xvii

Chapter 1: Willing to Become Free   1

Chapter 2: Become Brave Enough to Wonder   25

Chapter 3: Why We Run   45

Chapter 4: Hiding behind the Body   71

Chapter 5: Speaking the Unspeakable   93

Chapter 6: Don't Call Me Crazy   113

Chapter 7: Love Every Part   135

Chapter 8: Freeing What's Frozen   159

Chapter 9: Reparenting Yourself   175

Chapter 10: Happy Days Ahead   197

Resources   213

Endnotes   215

Index   217

About the Author   225

FOREWORD

When I graduated from college in 1971, the parts of me I showed to the world embraced the hippie, anti-establishment ethic of the day and helped me come across as carefree and uninterested in traditional routes to "success." Just beneath those parts, though, I was an anxious mess. Due to an undiagnosed case of ADHD, I had been a poor student throughout my academic career and had heard frequently about that from my driven, highly successful father's critical part. I was supposed to follow in his footsteps to become an accomplished physician. Instead, I was doing manual labor, hopping from painting houses to pounding spikes on the railroad, pretending to enjoy that life. All the while my inner critics were echoing my father at his worst. At my core I felt like the lazy, stupid loser those words conveyed. I had no idea what to do with my life.

Then I heard about Transcendental Meditation and did the weekend initiation. I found that with my mantra I could enter a state of peace and calm that I'd never felt before. I also felt a reassuring connection to something larger and was guided to the career path that I'm still on, 50 years later. I practiced TM devotedly for the next 10 years, until my clients started teaching me the basics of what has come to be the Internal Family Systems (IFS) model of psychotherapy, and I recognized the fear, worthlessness, and emotional pain carried by parts of me I needed to heal. I actively shifted to help those parts rather than avoid them.

For many years, Gabby Bernstein was dismissing her own exiled pain- and shame-filled parts through obsessive work. This bypassing through achievement and spirituality seemed (and probably was) better overall than her earlier drug and alcohol addiction, but it was no less a way to run from her exiled emotions. As she writes in this courageous book, "While I put down the drink and the drugs, I was still acting out in addictive ways in efforts to control the unconscious impermissible feelings that I couldn't possibly face. 'Wow, Gabby, you get so much done!' or 'You're so impressive!' It was not only socially acceptable to be a work addict, it was something people admired. . . . I thought, *This is who I am. I'm driven, I'm a worker, and I have an important job; I'm helping so many people.* I thought my behavior was healthy, but deep down it was just another addictive pattern 'protecting' me."

The success story Gabby was telling herself (and that everyone around her was telling her) kept her going and ignoring many signs from her body that everything wasn't so rosy, like TMJ and chronic gastrointestinal issues: "Buried beneath the successful story I'd created about my life was a terrified little girl."

I have now found buried beneath my own success story several little boys whom I'd left frozen amid past scenes of humiliation and loneliness, and I expect I'll find more as I keep examining the ways I'm still driven or distracted. To find and face them isn't easy; in fact, it can be the hardest work of your life. For Gabby, things shifted when she began to realize that the parts of her pushing her success story had created an unlivable life and began to wonder why. The answer she got when she asked inside was that she had been traumatized in ways that she had minimized or denied altogether.

We are fortunate that, in the past several decades, a number of effective approaches to treating trauma have evolved, and Gabby became so committed to that healing path that she tried most of them, including the work on physical pain of John Sarno, Peter Levine's Somatic Experiencing, the wise perspective of Dan Siegel, as well as EMDR, tapping (EFT) and acupuncture, medication, and self-compassion. At some point, Gabby's therapist started using the approach I developed, and I am very honored that the final chapters of this book movingly describe her IFS journey.

She found that she could honor the addictive, controlling, and rageful parts of her that had tried to protect her from feeling her pain. She could reassure them that, while she needed their services when she was young, she could handle that pain now, so they could relax. When she could love instead of disdain those protectors, they softened and became useful advisors rather than extreme automatic reactions. She could also witness where her hurt and scared exiles were stuck in the past and bring them back home to her loving presence.

For me, the following statement from Gabby reflects a depth of appreciation for my life's work that is very moving:

"For years I judged my protectors and couldn't even acknowledge my exiles. Today, with my newfound compassion and love for all my parts, I can easily forgive myself in the moment, notice the part, and turn to my resourced Self for support. Working with parts is a daily spiritual practice that changed my life forever."

Reading this book may not be easy for you because, like Gabby, you may begin to wonder why, with all the spiritual work you've done, you still have problematic impulses and behaviors. You may also find that your protectors mount a successful campaign to discredit the book or Gabby herself so you won't have to wonder. Exploring exiled pain or shame isn't for everyone.

In short, this book is an act of extreme courage. In being so vulnerable and honest in these pages, Gabby risked disaffecting her audience and her fellow spiritual leaders. But once we heal our burdens and access Self, we can't keep pretending. My hope is that this book inspires the spiritual world not only to heal our inner exiles, but also to change our society so there are fewer external exiles.

— Richard C. Schwartz, Ph.D.,
founder of Internal Family Systems therapy

ACKNOWLEDGMENTS

I thank my parents for helping me become the woman I am today.

Thank you to everyone who helped bring this book to life, my publishing team at Hay House and Audible, my editors Anne Barthel and Andrea Vinely Jewell. Thanks to my team for carrying the message. I thank my agents, Scott Hoffman and Steve Troha, for believing in this book. Thanks to my publicist Jessica Reda at Sarah Hall PR for your hard work spreading this message. I thank Jenny Sansouci for being my cheerleader throughout the writing process. And MaryAnn DiMarco for your endless guidance and support.

I want to thank Tammy Valicenti for your therapeutic support.

It wouldn't have been possible for me to write this book without the support of therapist Kachina Myers guiding my path.

Finally, I thank my husband, Zach, for caring deeply about this book.

INTRODUCTION

The Truth about This Book

"We're anxious for you, Gabby," said my publisher after reading the first pass of the manuscript.

"It feels too vulnerable," they continued. "You're revealing one difficult moment after the next. You're not showing your true strength."

"My ability to be this vulnerable *is* my true strength," I responded.

The conversation carried on with several moments of tears, passionate explanations defending the manuscript, mixed with mutual agreement and love.

While this was a challenging conversation to have, it was necessary. This book is different from the eight that came before. This book reveals parts of me that I'd never known were there until I started this writing process. This book tells the story of how to survive and thrive. This is my story of recovering from trauma.

This isn't a book filled with self-help tools offering a quick fix for your discomfort. Instead, it's a journey toward lifelong transformation filled with stories of resilience.

My hope is that my vulnerability will give you the chance to look more closely at yours. I hope to give you permission to face feelings you've buried deep, and give you guidance on how to heal from them. This book will help you reclaim the fragmented parts of who you are—your innocence, your faith, your ability to know true love within. It offers you the guided path to the peace you're looking for. My prayer is that this book sets you free.

So while this may not seem like my other books on manifesting, spirituality, and connecting to the Universe, it's actually my greatest spiritual book of all. The journey I underwent to get to where I am today, the methods I was led to for healing, and my resilient path are nothing short of a miracle. Every step of the way I was guided by a Universal presence of love by my side.

Spirit is in all of it. In the stories of heartache, fear, trauma, and dissociation. There's spirit in the therapeutic processes, methods, and practices shared. Every word in this book is infused with the love of the Universe to help you awaken to the greatest part of yourself, the source of love within you.

Living a spiritual life isn't about moving past the pain and suffering, but instead embracing it. When we honor our suffering we become safe enough to face the dark corners and bring them to the light. This isn't the easy path, but it offers miracles on the other side. When you open a book like this it means you're claiming a level of joy and peace you never knew were possible. I mean that with all of my heart. When you bravely follow my guidance, show up for the steps, and honor the feelings that come up along the way, you will come out the other side a new version of yourself. You will come through back to you.

When I was a kid, my family had a tradition around the dinner table. Instead of raising our glasses and saying "Cheers," we'd say, "Happy Days!" I don't remember how this tradition came to be, but it's a bittersweet memory I have of my family. I longed for happiness—but I don't believe I was truly happy because I didn't know inner peace or freedom.

Today, at the age of 42, with a lot of life behind me, I can see how *unhappy* those days were for me. I can see the long detour into fear that ultimately led me to my knees. I can see the young woman who surrendered to a spiritual path of recovery. I can see the author and spiritual teacher vulnerable onstage, speaking her truth to feel released from the past. I can see the brave woman who fearlessly showed up for herself in the pursuit of inner peace and freedom. I can see my journey to becoming new.

My commitment to this freedom has allowed me to raise my glass and truly know what it means to say, "Happy Days!"

Now it's your turn.

This is a journey of unlearning fear and remembering love. I'm guiding you every step of the way . . .

CHAPTER 1

Willing to Become Free

It's 8 A.M. in New York City. I'm sitting in my double-parked, beat-up white Toyota waiting for the street cleaners to sweep past me. I shield my eyes from the sunlight as I chug a red Gatorade. I'm dehydrated, nauseous, and still wired from the after-party that ended 30 minutes earlier. I'm a complete mess. Having not slept the night before, I have no business being behind the wheel even if it's just to adhere to the neighborhood parking rules.

I have to sit in the car for 30 more minutes before I can legally park. So I push a cassette into the tape player and press play. I've listened to this recording countless times. It's a recording from a psychic reading I'd had five months earlier. The psychic's first words are, "You're struggling with alcohol and drugs." I hear my voice quiver in response, "Well, it's not that bad." Within the next few minutes, she goes on to say, "My dear, you are able to exercise free will in this lifetime. And you are caught between two choices. You can choose to stay on your current path and severely struggle with drug addiction. Or you can choose to get clean and make a major impact on the world." I rewind the recording to hear it again. Then again.

Her words repeat in my head, "You can choose to stay on your current path and severely struggle with drug addiction. Or you can choose to get clean and make a major impact on the world." I hear her words, but I don't believe them. I cannot imagine a world free from addiction, let alone a world where I'm making a major impact.

I look at the clock: 8:30 A.M. The street cleaners should be arriving soon. As I listen to the psychic on repeat, I send a text to my business partner: "Hey, late night, I won't be in the office until noon." At 24, I own a nightlife PR firm. Getting to work at noon is no big deal. I rewind the tape and play it again. "You can choose to stay on your current path and severely struggle with drug addiction. Or you can choose to get clean and make a major impact on the world."

Outside the car, the noise of people walking toward the subway interrupts me. They look so put together with their coffee cups and shoulder bags. As I watch everyone begin their day, I accept that mine is ending. The street cleaners sweep through the lane across from me, and I follow them from behind to secure my spot. I leave my empty Gatorade bottle on the floor of my trashed car and head back into my apartment. I'm desperate to get into bed, but I have to wash my face from the night before. I jump in my moldy shower and let the water wash over me as my mascara runs down my face.

When I'm done showering, I quickly get into bed and take some kind of downer. While I wait for my sleeping pill to kick in, I feverishly journal the psychic's words over and over: "You can choose to stay on your current path and severely struggle with drug addiction. Or you can choose to get clean and make a major impact on the world." I write so that I don't have to face the severe anxiety and heart palpitations. As the pill sets in, the anxiety subsides as if it's being shut behind a door, one that will reopen when I wake. The sounds of the trash cans clashing outside my window and the people heading to work become softer and softer as I finally fall asleep.

As I recall that morning, I have tears in my eyes. I can think my way back into that car as if it were yesterday. I can connect to those feelings of shame, insecurity, and unsafety. I know that girl intimately, and I'm proud of the choice she made to be the woman she is today. Even though it would take her another year of self-destruction, addiction, and near death to finally get clean and sober, she let the path unfold perfectly. I thank God every day that she chose the path of recovery.

My 24-year-old self could never have imagined who I am today. Thankfully she made the right choice to get clean and hold a vision for a better future, for true happiness. A vision of freedom and inner peace.

Today that vision has become my reality. I'm free from my past because I became brave enough to face the deeper reasons behind my suffering and fearlessly show up for healing. And now I know the true meaning of peace in the present. I sit here in my office surrounded by a stack of spiritual books I've authored. My desk is adorned with affirmation cards, crystals, and a sonogram photo of my son, Oliver, when he was in utero. My husband, Zach, is downstairs playing with Oliver while I sit in my office, allowing the voice of freedom to move through me so that I can guide you toward freedom today.

I'm free from my past because
I became brave enough to face the
deeper reasons behind my suffering
and fearlessly show up for healing.

Guided by Spirit

The journey toward true inner peace begins with the willingness to hold a vision for a new way of living. No matter how much you've struggled or suffered, you have the power to hold a vision for a better life. When we claim that vision, we open an invisible door to receive spiritual support and intuitive guidance to help us manifest the change we desire. We begin the journey of undoing the fears from our past so that we can claim love, peace, and freedom in the present. *Undoing* is the operative word. Deep within all of us is a loving truth, but we've built up walls against it. Undoing the patterns, thought forms, and programming we were brought up to believe is what's required to return to the truth of who we are. There's nothing "out there" that can give us that love; it's already within us. We must dismantle the fear, trauma, and patterns that keep us stuck in the belief that peace is unattainable. Peace and love are who we are; we just forgot. I'm here to remind you that it's safe to reclaim that love and affirm that you are ready to live with more inner peace and freedom than you've ever thought possible. And it begins with your new vision for a better life. That vision is enough to set a transformational process in motion. A process that will guide you to freedom from the past and inner peace in the present.

My willingness to see beyond a world of limitation allowed me to begin the process of stepping into a better future. That willingness is what allowed me to heal myself so that I could help others heal and make an impact on the world. But before I could embrace a new vision for my life, I had to face the wounds of my past that were keeping me down.

It's a brave act to face your fears and past experiences. Many people spend a lifetime doing everything in their power to avoid past wounds. It's painful, scary, and even heartbreaking to accept the wounded parts of ourselves. And we can't do it alone. In order to go to the places that scare us we must be brave enough to ask for help. That help will come in many forms, from therapists to counselors, spiritual guides, and friends. Throughout this book I will introduce you to the help I received to claim my experience of freedom. But none of those forms of help could have been available to me if I hadn't turned to the most important place first, my spiritual faith.

I'd always believed in a Higher Power and felt drawn to spiritual principles and teachers. I intuitively knew that I had a connection to a source of love beyond my physical sight. Even in my darkest moments of addiction I had a stack of spiritual books next to my bed. My desire to know God ultimately was what saved my life. Without my spiritual faith and my pursuit to expand my inner awareness, I wouldn't have been able to survive some of the experiences I share in this book. My spirituality held me up, kept me safe, and directed my healing path.

In retrospect I can see how Spirit was guiding me every step of the way. Every therapist, yoga teacher, spiritual book, or healer was divinely planted into my life at the exact moments I needed them in order to take the next step on my journey. It was all divine guidance. I always had faith that Spirit was leading me, and that is what allowed me to show up as a teacher even when I didn't have it all together. And it was the source of inspiration that allowed me to feel safe enough to face the wreckage from my past so it could be healed.

My spirituality held me up, kept me safe, and directed my healing path.

Worthiness

At first it wasn't easy for me to face my past. Deep down, even though I didn't realize it at the time, what I was most afraid of was that I was unworthy of a life of happiness and peace. My formative experiences painted a worldview based on fear that separated me from the peace within.

The feeling of unworthiness is buried deep. Most people can't even identify it (it took me over a decade). I once gave a talk in front of hundreds of spiritual entrepreneurs. These were people who had devoted their lives to personal growth and spiritual development, and they were committed to helping others do the same. They arrived at the event thinking that I was going to teach them methods for promoting their work or growing their spiritual business. They were wrong; they were in for something much more important.

My talk that day was all about worthiness. In the opening of my talk, I proclaimed that the only reason they were blocked from the success, abundance, or whatever it was that they wanted was because they didn't believe they were worthy of it. The audience protested at first because this was an alarming concept to people who had previously identified as confident and influential. But what they weren't yet facing was that the blocks in their way weren't because of the outside world, but lingering feelings of unworthiness.

When I speak of worthiness, I'm not talking about being worthy of money, or romance, or a career advancement. I'm speaking of being worthy of love. Early in my therapeutic recovery, my therapist explained to me that behind all of my blocks and fear were the feelings of being unlovable and inadequate. It took a moment for that to sink in. At first I wanted to resist her because I'd built up a worldview of my life that convinced me I was very adequate and loved. As time went on in my therapy, I was able to look closer. I could see that underneath all of my credentials, love from fans, and my seemingly positive self-perception was a traumatized little girl who thought she was unworthy. I started noticing the moments when I would actually say out loud to myself, "I'm just a piece of shit." Previously I had brushed these moments under the rug. But the more I shined light on them, the more apparent it became to me that I was indeed suffering from the core wound of feeling unlovable and inadequate.

As I continued to unpack my therapist's theory, I started to witness all the ways I'd avoided feeling unlovable and inadequate. I spent decades anesthetizing those feelings with drugs, romantic relationships, work, food, and any form of outside validation. I could see how I was running and the core wounds that I was running from. And these wounds continued to be perpetuated throughout my life.

Looking deeper

When we have core beliefs of unworthiness, they will manifest in every corner of our lives. In order to undo that belief, we must look at what's behind it. The spiritual teachers Abraham-Hicks say, "A belief is really only a thought that you keep thinking." The fear-based thoughts that turn into beliefs of unworthiness often show up in early childhood. When we are children, the world presents us with experiences that separate us from our worthiness and we build up thoughts that we're not good enough, we're different, or we're unsafe. When these fear-based thoughts are not fully processed, they become a story line that we repeat over and over until it becomes a belief.

No matter how seemingly happy or blatantly painful our childhood was, those early experiences have influenced the way we live. Throughout the book I will guide you to look more closely at how your childhood experiences affect your life. When we're looking more closely at these experiences, I'll reference a word that can be very triggering. That word is *trauma*. There's Trauma with a *big T* and trauma with a *small t*. Typically people associate trauma with big issues like sexual assault, abuse, severe neglect, or death in the family—trauma with a *big T*. Trauma with a *big T* can occur when someone is exposed to varied and multiple traumatic events, often of an invasive nature or natural disasters, medical injuries, hospitalization, school violence, and loss. Early childhood trauma encompasses the painful experiences that occur to children ages zero to six. Trauma with a *small t*, on the other hand, can be a highly distressing but nonthreatening experience that goes unrecognized. Some examples of *small t* trauma include being bullied, the death of a pet, emotional abuse or harassment, or losing an important relationship.

From a spiritual perspective, the painful experiences we had as kids were fractures in our energetic connection to the love within us (or the God within). Each minor (or major) fracture, such as being bullied or feeling unsafe, separated us further and further from the source of love. In some cases of Trauma with a *big T*, the fractures can be so severe that the child grows up living in a constant state of fear. Each fracture adds up and distances us further from our connection to spirit and love.

No matter how seemingly happy
or blatantly horrible our childhood was,
we all have had painful experiences
that influence the way we live.

Childhood neglect and trauma (with a *big T* or a *small t*) has a proven effect on the brain. A child's brain development is directly affected by the type of attachment they receive from their parents.[1] A secure attachment helps the child's problem-solving part of the brain develop properly, while allowing them to process emotions in a healthy way. With a secure attachment a child knows that it's safe to return to their loving parent when they're afraid. This sense of safety with a primary caregiver helps the child develop a greater sense of trust in love, whereas a child who's experienced poor attachment due to abuse, neglect, etc., may not develop as fully the problem-solving areas of the brain and may, therefore, act out in undesirable ways. Poor attachment can lead a child to struggle with coping, social engagement skills, problem solving, tantrums, and the inability to self-regulate. A child with poor attachment does not have an anchor back to love and therefore feels alone in the world.

Many of you reading this right now may be thinking, luckily, *I didn't experience any type of trauma. I can't relate to this.* But *small t* trauma can be a single incident of being bullied on the playground, a teacher calling you stupid, a public humiliation in the cafeteria, or the passive neglect of not getting your needs met in the first years of your life. And these, too, can have a real impact. We don't necessarily realize, for instance, how hurtful it was for us if our mother was constantly stressed or if our parents were emotionally unavailable. Whether a child suffers either form of trauma (*big T* or *small t*), the end result can be deep-rooted unconscious pain and feeling unworthy of love.

Maybe you grew up in a household with financial insecurity, so you believe you'll always live in lack. Or maybe you experienced neglect as a child and today you feel unworthy of a loving relationship. Or maybe you thought that your childhood was perfect, but deep down you know you're struggling with feelings of not being seen and heard. Our early childhood experiences become the driving force behind the way we live as adults. And those painful events contribute to the feelings of being unlovable and inadequate. Many people are aware of the ways that their childhood experiences play a role in who they have become, but they still write it off thinking, *Well, that was just in the past; it's over now*; or we tend to believe that it's now just *who we are*. What we don't realize is that the shadows from the past are replayed in the present and projected onto the future until we awaken to a healing path.

Dismissal of the past stems from the fact that it can often feel too painful to look back. In other cases, we can go through life not remembering the experiences that contributed to the feelings or beliefs we have about ourselves today. From infancy to the present, we've been avoiding these feelings of unworthiness with all kinds of addictive patterns and avoidance tactics. We will do anything to avoid feeling unlovable or inadequate. In addition to exiling the impermissible feelings of unworthiness, we look for the lost love in all the wrong places. We look for love in relationships, in praise, and even at the bottom of a bottle. We believe that something outside of us will provide the love we cannot find within. But when we become safe enough to face the feelings from the past, we can reconnect to the loving presence that never left us. That's the journey we are embarking on now.

We're all in this together

Whether we've experienced trauma with a *big T* or a *small t*, we've all experienced suffering. And while that suffering may have seemed like a moment in time, it lives in our subconscious and in our body, informing every thought and every action. The core underlying perceptions of being unlovable or inadequate play into our career path, romantic relationships, and even how we handle stress. These deep-rooted feelings will be addressed in depth later, but they must be called out here.

Many of us are able to coexist with these unconscious feelings because we built coping mechanisms to manage them. Several of the ways we've mitigated our underlying pain have often been socially acceptable. For instance, drinking to fall asleep at night, always being in a romantic relationship, or working to the point of burnout. In some cases, coping mechanisms look like praise-worthy behavior.

For me, getting sober was only the first step to recovery. In the early days of my sobriety, I didn't have the tools for healing the root cause of my addiction. In fact, I didn't even know a deeper wound existed. So while I put down the drink and the drugs, I was still acting out in addictive ways in efforts to control the unconscious impermissible feelings that I couldn't possibly face. I became a work addict. And I was praised for it! People would say things like, "Wow, Gabby, you get so much done!" or "You're so impressive!" It was not only socially acceptable to be a work addict, but it was something people admired. All the while I was avoiding true healing because it was too terrifying to face my unconscious pain.

Of course, I didn't realize that at the time. I thought, *This is who I am. I'm driven, I'm a worker, and I have an important job; I'm helping so many people.* I thought my behavior was healthy, but deep down it was just another addictive pattern "protecting" me. It's important to call this out, as you may not identify with having destructive patterns. But take a moment to look at your socially acceptable patterns and how they may be a way to avoid deeper feelings. Do you obsess about everything you eat and in return get praise from others for how good you look? Are you giving so much to others that you give up all of your time? Often deeper feelings are hard to uncover. For now, you don't have to know what those deeper feelings are. I simply want to encourage you to notice where something feels off inside you and when you turn to certain activities, comforts, or people to numb uncomfortable feelings. This simple noticing is a small step toward discovering what's deeper.

In 2020 in the face of the COVID-19 pandemic, the world experienced a trauma together that activated everyone on an individual level. Forced to slow down, stay home, and isolate, we were left with ourselves. Feeling out of control often triggers those impermissible feelings we've spent our lives running from. Many of you reading this right now may have been unaware of your unresolved pain and suffering before the pandemic, only to be totally triggered and out of control when the world shut down. During the pandemic, I received hundreds of messages from people throughout the world suffering with depression, anxiety, addiction, and chronic pain. When we slow down and become still, our deep-rooted pain comes to the surface for healing. The body naturally wants to repair itself and psychological repair sets in too. But if we lack the tools for identifying and healing trauma and the therapeutic resources to free us from the past, we become frozen in the terror of facing our suffering.

Protecting ourselves

My therapist taught me to recognize the ways I've built up forms of protection. She called these "the protector" parts of myself. My "protector" parts attack back when I feel threatened, or I immediately try to fix things when I feel out of control. One of my "protectors" had a mantra that I paraphrased from my favorite hip-hop music: "If you mess with me, now it's a must that I mess with you." I know it sounds dramatic and silly, but it was literally a fighting attitude that I hid behind. My lack of safety as a child led me to always feel unsafe. Therefore, I built up a shield of protection to avoid ever feeling the sadness and disappointment of not being cared for or loved. We all have "protectors" that work really hard in an attempt to keep us safe. But in order to truly be free, we must ask the protectors to step aside so that we can create space for spiritual healing and therapeutic guidance back to the resourced loving presence within. This book will be your guide to laying down your extreme protection mechanisms so that you can allow the spirit of love to step in and guide you back to peace. In time you'll feel safe and cared for through your own ability to love and support yourself unconditionally.

It may seem hard to contemplate what freedom and peace could look like. If you were to ask me 15 years ago what freedom and happiness were, I would have said something entirely different from the freedom I know today. I couldn't have even contemplated the relief, joy, and inner peace that I have cultivated. I couldn't see what freedom was because I didn't know yet what stood in the way of it. But I had a willingness to be free and that was enough.

While you won't feel worthy of love overnight, trust that going on the journey through this book will heal the false perceptions of being unlovable and inadequate. For today, all I ask is that you stay willing to feel free, pay attention to the ways you may feel unworthy of that freedom, and witness and honor your experiences from that past. I don't want you to get overwhelmed. Instead, be proud of yourself for having the willingness to look for the ways you may be caught in unresolved fear and feelings of unworthiness.

Even if you don't realize it, you are willing to live in a new way. It's your willingness that guided you to pick up this book. It's your willingness that opened your consciousness to see the book advertised online, or to listen to your friend who suggested it, or to finally pick it up off the shelf. The slightest willingness to feel better is a prayer to the Universe asking for help and an acceptance that there has to be a better way. Unconsciously or consciously, you've set the intention to open up to a new freedom and peace. As long as you stay connected to that intention, you will be guided every step of the way.

That is my promise.

If any of the principles in this book, whether they be spiritual or psychological, happen to trigger you in some way, do not stop reading. This is a journey of facing the truth of who you are, and that truth can be uncomfortable at first. But I assure you, it's far more uncomfortable to hide it. You're reading this now, you're willing to witness your resistance, and you're ready to be at peace. If at any point you feel that you need further support and therapeutic guidance, visit DearGabby.com/HappyResources.

Your spiritual guidance system

I've been brave enough to witness my fear, and I've had one way of working through it that never failed me: honor my experience and surrender it to a spiritual guidance system. Even early in my sobriety when I didn't yet have a strong spiritual foundation, I was willing to surrender my fear to something beyond me. I remember my sober mentor suggested that I get on my knees and pray. "To who?" I said. "Whoever or whatever you want," she responded. At the time it didn't matter whether or not I knew who or what I was praying to. What mattered was my willingness to humbly ask for help. And that's what I'll say to you today. When I suggest you pray, you don't have to know who or what you're praying to. All you have to do is be willing to turn over your fears to a presence or power greater than you. If spirituality is new or uncomfortable to you, then call it by a different name, like the Universe or Spirit or *love*. Think of this as establishing a greater connection to an inner compass or voice of love. Throughout the book, I will guide you to release control to a spiritual presence. With that in mind, I want to honor you for whatever your spiritual, religious, or personal growth path may be. I'm here to help you become open to inviting a spiritual presence or love into your consciousness to help you surrender to the path ahead.

Throughout this book, I will guide you to establish a spiritual connection of your own understanding. A connection that will give you strength and hope as you embark on the healing practices that follow. Although in the coming chapters I will lean on neuroscience and life-changing psychological approaches to aid your healing, a spiritual connection will be your lighthouse throughout this process. I've relied on my spiritual connection to be the steady force of love that kept me moving forward in my pursuit of freedom. I want this for you too.

Most of us live life trying to control our circumstances in order to feel safe. When we catastrophize, obsess over fearful thoughts, or feel an unconscious sense of anxiety, these behaviors are subconscious ways of trying to control our circumstances. Whenever we try to control everything, we are not going to feel at peace. A true state of peace comes when we are willing to give over our plans and trust in a Higher Power. When we invite a spiritual presence to help us, we can let ourselves off the hook. Developing a relationship with a Higher Power, God, the Universe, or the voice of love is a decision to let go and be guided.

We can choose at any moment to release control to a Higher Power by letting go of the rope. This practice may sound simple, but it's challenging for the fearful parts of ourselves that want to hold on tightly to some semblance of control.

Surrendering your need to control comes through prayer. It doesn't matter if you've never prayed before, or if you don't know who or what you're praying to, think of the following prayer as setting an intention to surrender:

Thank you, Universe, for guiding me on this path to becoming new. I honor this vision of how I want to feel. I am willing to receive guidance now.

Now take a moment to pause and feel what it's like to turn over your control to a Higher Power or inner voice of love. Honor *what is* and *what was* and hold a vision for *what can be*.

Honor your suffering

Feeling genuine inner peace and freedom isn't something many people are familiar with. I've spent my entire career witnessing the suffering of others. I've led talks throughout the world, and no matter what country I'm in, people are suffering silently. Even if your outside conditions seem excellent, there's probably an inner disturbance begging to be repaired.

We must be willing to accept this truth: we all suffer. Bringing loving awareness to our suffering is part of the solution. The Zen master Thich Nhat Hanh says, "When we know how to suffer, we suffer much, much less."[2] To me this means that when we know how to honor our feelings of suffering, we can allow them to move through us rather than resist them. It's our resistance to suffering that keeps us silent, alone, and afraid. It's okay to admit that you've struggled or are struggling. In fact, it's freeing to get honest about it. Calling it out and naming it can bring real relief. Give yourself permission to be going through a tough time or to acknowledge a past trauma, big or small. Honor your feelings and your experience. Many of us didn't grow up with parents or adults who honored our feelings. That's all the more reason why we must do that for ourselves right now. When we learn to embrace our suffering, we can honor our pain and transform our perception of it.

A few simple words will help you come to peace with where you are. The words *There has to be a better way* are a prayer for a miracle. These words invoke a journey of undoing your fears from the past so that you can claim freedom and peace in the present. You don't even need to know or understand your subconscious fears. All that matters is that you believe there can be a better way to live.

Try saying these words out loud: "There has to be a better way." Those simple words opened me up to receive the guidance to get clean and sober. My willingness to accept that life didn't have to be so hard was what I needed to open the door to a new vision for my life.

The words *There has to be a better way*
are a prayer for a miracle.

Create a vision for a new life

Having a vision for a better life isn't about a certain amount of money in the bank, a special love partner, or a credential. I'm talking about a vision for how you want to feel when you wake up each day. In my early sobriety, I couldn't contemplate what a better life could look like, but I knew one thing for sure: I wanted to wake up without anxiety, excited to live another day. Knowing how I wanted to feel became the backbone of my journey toward peace. I was never aiming for special recognition or accomplishment, so I didn't have to rely on the outside world to show me the way. My vision was about how I wanted to feel. And how I feel is something I have always had the power to change. So do you.

So now I want to ask you, what is your vision? In answering this, forget what you think you need and instead focus on how you want to feel. Maybe it's hard for you to even ponder what it could look like to feel a different way. Or maybe you're blocked by feelings of fear or unworthiness. Try for a moment to suspend your disbelief and give yourself full permission to dream of how you want to feel in your life. Answer this question quickly in a journal: "How do I want to feel?" Don't think, just let your pen flow, capturing all the feelings you want to experience.

Find some uninterrupted time in your day to do some freewriting. At the top of the page, ask yourself, "How do I want to feel, and what would that look like?" Then just write. Let whatever comes to your mind move through you. Be open to receiving this vision statement with clarity. Again, we are aiming for a feeling, not an outcome like a job or a credential or a title. Try not to let your vision be reliant on someone or something. For instance, you may feel tempted to hold a vision of a deep romantic partnership, thinking that that will make you feel complete. While there's nothing wrong with wanting romance, that freedom in romance cannot come until you assume the feeling of freedom on your own. You may want that romance to feel safe, connected, or at ease. But safety, connection, and ease must come from you first. Committing to how you want to feel, and accepting that it cannot come from an outside force, is the secret to manifesting the great changes you are here to make.

Give yourself permission to believe in a new vision of how you can feel even if you can't see how you'll get there. Keep it simple. Just envision what it would be like to have the feelings you want. A vision statement can be something like, "I feel relaxed and easygoing. I feel safe in my body. I open my arms and fearlessly welcome whatever unfolds." Or it might be as simple as, "I wake up without anxiety every day." Holding the vision of how you want to feel will set you up to receive the exact guidance you need to get there. This vision opens you up to infinite possibilities for great change and growth. And because it's based on a feeling rather than an outside source, it makes the possibilities for your life limitless.

Give yourself permission to believe in a new vision even if you can't see how you'll get there.

Now that you have a vision statement, consider what it reveals about feelings you may have been avoiding or something deep inside you that needs to be healed. For me, realizing I wanted to wake up without anxiety every day made the anxiety I was living with much more apparent. And this motivated me to dig deeper into that feeling of living without anxiety. So what might your vision statement reveal about deeper feelings?

Once you've written your vision statement, say it out loud a few times. See how it makes you feel to put it into spoken words. You'll know you've established it when you feel good saying it out loud.

Now, it's important to realize that a part of you may resist your new vision. This brings us back to unworthiness and that part of you that doesn't believe you're worthy of peace and freedom. That part of you that doesn't believe you can feel safe without a romantic partner or a certain amount of money or at a specific body weight. Remember, that is the part of you that became fractured and disconnected from love. It's the voice of fear within you. Acknowledge that fear and say nice things to it, such as, "I witness my resistance, and I honor the fearful part of me. I am willing to feel {insert your desired feeling here}." Talking back to your resistance with love is a form of acceptance that dissolves the fear. Many of us are used to shutting down parts of ourselves and listening only to other parts. But throughout this book I will help you learn to listen with love. Each practice in this book is designed to remind you of the voice of love within you. Follow my guidance and return to the love of who you are. Be kind to yourself, be patient, and trust the plan ahead. The beauty here is that you don't have to figure out how to make your vision happen. Continue reading this book and trust that the path will unfold.

Now let's return to your prayer. Read this prayer again and then pause:

Thank you, Universe, for guiding me on this path to becoming new. I honor this vision of how I want to feel. I am willing to receive guidance now.

A simple prayer allows a spiritual connection of your own understanding to set in. Throughout the book, I will help you strengthen that connection so you feel safe and guided to your new vision and how you want to feel. There is a presence of spiritual guidance that is devoted to each and every one of us. Each time we commit to feeling good and are willing to change, Spirit can step in. You'll begin to feel this spiritual presence show up in your life often in the form of intuition. Maybe you'll be reading a chapter of the book and feel a strong desire to try out one of the methods I recommend. That intuition is Spirit guiding you to the exact modality that could change your life forever. My constant commitment to feel better is what helped me stay open to receiving the spiritual guidance that was always available to me. When you make your own commitment to how you want to feel, and remain willing to do what it takes to get there, you can know that Spirit is by your side.

As we move forward, I will ask you to look closely at patterns and feelings that may be uncomfortable. If you ever feel challenged to continue on, return to the prayer above. Write it on a Post-it or note card. Revisit it daily to help you stay in contact with spiritual guidance so that you know and affirm you're not alone on this journey. If prayer is new to you, then consider this a form of intention setting. Say the same prayer, but omit the first sentence. Instead, say:

I honor this vision of how I want to feel. I am willing to receive guidance now.

My willingness to get clean and sober and my vision of waking up without anxiety was enough to set me on the path to become the woman I am today. My willingness to become new and my daily practice of surrender is what got me here.

You don't need to figure out how you'll get "there." Focus on feeling peaceful, then the rest will follow. This is all about accepting that nothing outside of yourself can help you feel freedom and peace. This is a journey inward, not an outward action. The promise of inner peace is better than any material possession. By placing your feelings above all else you make your energy a priority. In order to manifest the life we want, we must first assume this desired positive energy. Initially, it's our feelings that create this, not our actions. Feeling joy and peace is what puts you in a place of attraction to living a life beyond your wildest dreams. Stay focused on the feeling rather than the outcome and you will be amazed by what unfolds.

Surrender one step at a time

Surrender your old story and become willing to embrace a new one. Respect what is in front of you and surrender to your vision statement now. Stay willing and trust what unfolds next.

Even the morning of writing this chapter I relied on surrender. I drove to a doctor's appointment with my mask at the ready due to the coronavirus pandemic. We were only two and a half months into social distancing and stay-at-home orders. I had a bag filled with hand sanitizer and rubber gloves. The world around me was out of control, uncertainty was at an all-time high, and I was trying to get pregnant. Instead of listening to the news, I chose to listen to an interview with the spiritual author Michael Singer. At one point in the interview Singer said, "To let the 'flow of life' be in charge means we first put aside our made-up preferences and respect what is unfolding in front of us. First respect it, then with love and compassion, raise it as it passes by you. That is how you become open to life's gifts." Singer's words were so meaningful to me at that moment. The idea of respecting what is in front of me felt like the most radical act of surrender. Surrender requires acceptance of the past, presence in the moment, and faith in the future. When we respect this moment, we become free from the judgment we place upon ourselves and our experiences.

One day at a time I have patiently developed a new relationship with myself. Over time I've learned to care for myself in the ways that I wasn't cared for. I've learned how to undo the feelings of being inadequate and unlovable. I've become safe in my body and my mind. I have learned to rely on a Higher Power to support my healing. And I've stepped into a new freedom and happiness. I feel that freedom deeply within my body. I feel safe, I feel confident, and I feel certain that my life is unfolding in miraculous ways. Each day I surrender through prayer and allow the Universe to show me what to do. This is what I know works, so this is what I do. When I listen to the wisdom that is within me, I can lean into uncertainty with ease. This is the promise, my friend: a path toward peace and freedom and the way to true happiness.

Freedom doesn't come overnight, but it comes when you're consistent. Each time you read a page of this book, you're taking a small action toward honoring your feelings, dismantling your coping mechanisms, and transforming your history so that you can be free.

I remember sitting in my first 12-step meeting 15 years ago, only days sober with the willingness to get clean. At the beginning of the meeting, the group read promises out loud. One of the promises that stood out most for me was, "We are going to know a new freedom and a new happiness." Those were the only words I took in the entire meeting. But they were enough to inspire me to stay clean and keep coming back. Today I'm promising the same to you. Keep showing up for this book, and the book will show up for you. Each page will guide you closer to "a new freedom and a new happiness."

Today, I woke up without anxiety. I woke up excited to get to my desk and write this book. I woke up proud of myself for all that I have healed and all that I can contribute. I can still hear the words of the psychic in the back of my mind, "You can choose to stay on your current path and severely struggle with drug addiction. Or you can choose to get clean and make a major impact on the world." I made a choice that set me free.

CHAPTER 2

Become Brave Enough to Wonder

I put down the drink and the drugs and picked up a boyfriend. Getting sober didn't mean that my addictive patterns went away. I transferred my addiction onto romantic relationships, food, work, and other vices that seemed socially acceptable. While I was deeply devoted to my spiritual path, recovery groups, and meditation practice, I was far from "recovered." In fact, now that I was clean, I was no longer able to deny or ignore my huge unspeakable fear: being alone. My codependent addiction was probably the worst addiction of all. I relied on romantic relationships to make me feel safe, lovable, and adequate. And when a relationship would end, I would immediately replace it with a new one.

Underneath the codependency was a core belief that I was not safe. So I turned my romantic relationships into my source of safety. I thought that a partner could fix my pain and make me whole. I turned my boyfriends into God. The fear of not having a boyfriend was so debilitating that I spent years in relationships with people who weren't right for me simply to avoid being alone. Being alone made me feel like

I was going to die. Whenever I faced a breakup, it would trigger a state of panic and I'd jump right into a new relationship to manage that impermissible fear. I worked hard to justify my codependent behavior because deep down it was too shameful to face. I defended that behavior in the same way I had defended my (pre-sober) drinking and drugging. In fact, it was a lot easier to admit that I was a drug addict than to admit that I was codependent.

Codependency wasn't the only new addiction replacing the drugs. I was also a workaholic. After getting sober, I embarked on a career as a motivational speaker and self-help author. My own spiritual devotion is what allowed me to teach from a place of authenticity and share vulnerably about my path. I became a raconteur, speaking to strangers about my journey of personal transformation. In fact, the more honest I was about my shortcomings—and no matter how ugly the truth—the more I could serve others because they could identify themselves in me. My work was created out of inspired spiritual action and a commitment to serve. When I was working I felt Spirit move through me, I felt connected to a Higher Power, I felt in tune with the love I'd always longed for. Without realizing it though, my work became another way I tried to stay safe and run from feeling the impermissible. Despite the genuine love for my work and service-driven mission, my working style was another addictive form of seeking relief from my suffering.

The search for relief

I believe that the root cause of addiction is the impermissible memories and feelings from the past, otherwise known as trauma. We run from our unresolved experiences and get caught on the hamster wheel of searching for relief.

That relief comes in many forms. Drugs and alcohol, sure. But there are a number of behaviors that are less frequently identified as a form of addiction. We commonly don't identify acceptable and productive habits, such as working overtime, a strict healthy lifestyle, even obsessive exercise, as a form of addiction. But when those habits become extreme behaviors, they are merely another way we run.

Addiction is a temporary form of relief for an addict—relief from the core wounds of the past. An addict will turn to their drug of choice (socially acceptable or not) to anesthetize their suffering in an effort to forget about the past and experience relief in the present. The sad reality is that the relief is fleeting and leads to greater pain and suffering.

Or addicts can replace one addiction with another and leave untouched the underlying condition. This is why the disease of addiction cannot be treated with abstinence alone. It must be addressed at the root level of emotional distress and energetic disturbances.

An addict will turn to their drug of choice (socially acceptable or not) to anesthetize their momentary suffering in an effort to forget about the past and experience relief in the present.

I ran for a decade. I ran in and out of relationships in order to feel safe. I ran from accomplishment to accomplishment to feel adequate. And I ran by controlling every area of my life to numb the feelings of fear that lived in my subconscious. The more I ran, the less I had to feel. The interesting thing is that I had no idea the real reason I was running.

My suffering was deep below the surface; therefore, I was subconsciously running from fear and toward anything that would give me a sense of control or security. I thought it was normal to work to the point of burnout. I thought it was acceptable to always have a boyfriend and/or fear being alone. I thought it was "funny" that I was controlling and super type A.

It was hard to even notice how fast I was running because it paralleled the rise of my career. Every year my audiences grew larger, my public profile expanded, and I stayed sober.

By the time I was 35, I had published five books and appeared on *Super Soul Sunday* with Oprah, who named me "a new thought leader for the next generation." I was married and running a big business that allowed me to travel all over the world, leading talks and meeting fans. On top of that I was hosting a regular radio show, creating weekly video blogs, generating a newsletter, recording digital learning products, appearing in the press, leading live workshops, and on and on.

While successes continued to manifest in my outer world, my inner world was hard to maintain. I lived in a constant state of fight, flight, or freeze, always on the lookout for something to go wrong. I only felt safe when I thought I was in control of my circumstances.

I'd spend every summer vacation in the library writing my next book and working hard to meet self-imposed deadlines. During the holidays, I'd sneak away to the back of my in-laws' house to find time to write. I remember each year my father-in-law would look at me and say, "Gabby, do you ever take a day off?" This made me feel defensive and I would quickly justify my behavior: "I love my work, and I'm helping a lot of people. How is that a problem?" And I did love my work. When I was working, I felt safe, inspired, and connected to other humans. But it's also where I felt most in control. I called the shots, I didn't have a boss, and no one could tell me what to do. I didn't have to rely on lots of people to help me. I didn't have to fear the inevitable disappointment if someone didn't show up in the right way. In fact, it was only when I was working that security would momentarily set in.

The harder I worked, the more praise I received from my contemporaries, publishers, friends, and family. I wore my successes like a badge of honor and told anyone who would listen about the work I did in the world. I desperately needed to validate my existence. While my true commitment to my work wasn't about the validation, it was at the time something I deeply needed to feel good enough and adequate.

The toll it took

All addictions take a toll at some point, even the seemingly acceptable ones. Whatever we do on an extreme and unconscious level will inevitably catch up with us. Addiction takes us out of the present and inevitably disturbs our nervous system, as well as our physical and emotional condition. The work addiction started to take a toll on my body.

Whatever we do on an extreme and unconscious level will inevitably catch up with us.

The constant deadlines, responsibilities, and commitments became impossible to hold together. I lived in a consistent state of hyperarousal, which created a lot of physical tension. I broke teeth because of extreme TMJ (temporomandibular joint syndrome), I was in and out of doctors' offices trying to diagnose my chronic gastrointestinal issues, and I lived in a constant state of physical discomfort. I was looking for an allopathic solution to my physical problems. Whenever a doctor would suggest that stress was a contributor, I'd agree and remind them that I was a spiritual teacher with a daily meditation practice. But then I'd immediately ask for the diet plan to heal my gut or the mouthguard to fix my TMJ. I wasn't yet safe enough to address the root cause. I was still running from an unresolved fear that I wasn't even aware of.

All the while I continued to do weekly therapy, deep meditation practices, and spiritual development. My spiritual practices and therapy were always there to guide me back to relief, but that temporary relief wasn't enough to sustain the way I was living. I was stuck in a cycle of work addiction that would lead to burnout. At that point, I'd hit my knees and surrender. Then I'd meditate, pray, and do personal growth work to peel myself off the floor.

I was so unaware of the ways that I was running that I often acted like nothing was wrong. In my therapy sessions, I'd sit on the sofa across from my therapist and talk about all the great things going on in my life. Whenever she'd challenge me to look more closely at my feelings and patterns, I'd shut down. I didn't understand it at the time, but being challenged to witness the vulnerable parts of myself was terrifying. Buried beneath the successful story I'd created about my life was a terrified little girl, dissociated from her past, unaware of what she was running from. And ironically, being in the presence of someone whose job it was to care for me didn't feel safe. In truth, I dreaded those sessions because they challenged me to face feelings I wasn't yet ready to reveal.

Vulnerability was a funny thing for me. Despite how hard it was for me to be vulnerable in therapy or relationships, it was easy when I spoke in front of audiences of strangers. When I was leading a live talk was when I felt most connected to God. The moment I stepped onto the stage I aligned with the truest part of who I am, the love of who I am, the joy of being alive, and the genuine desire to help others establish their own spiritual connection. Speaking onstage I became a channel for love and a conduit for spiritual awakening in others. The stage was my safe place where I could stand spiritually naked in my authentic truth.

One night I gave a talk in front of 2,000 people. From the moment I stepped onto the stage, I was open, free, and extremely authentic. I was totally fearless, vulnerable, and willing to share my truth no matter what. I told personal, shameful stories, I cried messy tears, and I showed the most authentic side of myself.

Ironically, despite how hard it was for me to be vulnerable in relationships, it was easy when I spoke in front of audiences of strangers.

That night onstage I saw my husband in the audience. He was smiling with pride, laughing at my jokes, and winking at me during the Q&A when I caught his eye. When I got off the stage, he said, "Wow, that was incredible." He looked at me with such pride. Returning to the hotel room several hours later, the energy between us changed. The vulnerable, authentic, open, and free woman was gone. And Zach was left with a different part of me. The part of me that was anxious, disconnected, and aloof. This was a common scenario.

I had no trouble being free and inspired onstage; that's when I felt safely connected to Spirit. But when I stepped off the stage, I would enter back into the part of myself that was scared and desperate to stay in control.

I was confronted with my need to control in 2015 when Zach and I decided we were ready to try to have a baby. At the same time, Zach had left his 10-year career in banking to run my business. He was highly qualified for the job, and I desperately needed his help. While all of this was full of exciting potential, it was terrifying to me. I had to give up a certain amount of control. If I were to be a mother, how would I work the way I'd been working? If I were to allow Zach to run the business, how would I maintain the level of authority that made me feel safe? All of this inquiry consumed my thoughts, although I never allowed myself to say it out loud. I didn't want to admit to myself—or anyone else—that I was terrified.

No one can run forever

My resistance to releasing control continued to manifest in my body. I started having panic attacks, numbness in my limbs, brain fog, and worsening gastrointestinal issues. Days would go by when I'd try to hold it together only to wind up in tears, saying over and over, "I can't go on like this!"

And I couldn't.

Ultimately, my cries for help were loud prayers to the Universe. My mantra was, "I can't go on like this; there has to be a better way." My spiritual practice was strong, I had a beautiful husband and a thriving business. Why was I so afraid all the time? There was no clear explanation for what was going on. This is when I started to wonder. I wondered why I had become a drug addict. I wondered why I suffered from anxiety, panic attacks, other addictions, and depression. I wondered why it was so hard for me to be vulnerable in my close relationships. I wondered why I so deeply suffered with codependency and the ever-present longing to feel good enough. I wondered what I was running from. My willingness to witness the chaos and become open to a better path was a prayer.

My bravery to wonder is what allowed me to ever so slightly surrender some control and let down my guard. Wondering why I was suffering allowed the truth to be revealed. Even though it would take several more months of meltdowns and panic attacks to recover the true reasons why I was running, the inquiry was enough to put me on a true healing path.

> When we become brave enough to wonder what we're running from or fighting against, we begin to undo the patterns that keep us stuck.

Become brave enough to wonder

When we become brave enough to wonder what we're running from or fighting against, we're inviting the Universe to step in and guide our healing path. Within all of us are exiled feelings, unresolved experiences, and memories that we think go away with time. But they cannot just go away. They deserve to be seen, cared for, and loved so that they can truly heal. Our fear of facing the emotions from our past gives them more power. Unresolved emotions affect every corner of our lives without us realizing it. We build up coping mechanisms and addictive patterns to avoid the pain of revisiting these feelings, memories, and experiences. Each coping strategy is a way to run from the emotions that can be triggered at any moment. Triggers like being rejected, being helpless or feeling out of control, or being blamed or shamed are among the many things that activate our deep-rooted suffering. The trigger activates the feeling, and an alarm goes off in our brain. Then we hide, run, or fight! We pick up the drink, binge on the food, text an ex-lover, start a new project—anything to hide from, run from, or push down the feelings we so desperately want to avoid.

The problem isn't just that we're running, but that we are unwilling to face what we're running from, and why. Uncovering these emotions must be done slowly and gently. You can't rip off the Band-Aid too fast. Some of these feelings have a long history and therefore take time to feel into.

Early childhood experiences mold the way we will live as adults. In an ideal world, a child would spend their earliest years in nurturing environments with strong attachment bonds. When a child feels safe and nurtured by their surroundings, it fosters optimal brain development and a sense of inner safety that supports their ability to effectively navigate the world. As infants and young children, we rely on our primary caregivers to keep us safe and alive. In fact, we come into the world biologically preprogrammed to establish a strong attachment bond with our caregivers so that we can survive.

It may be too overwhelming at this point to contemplate the ways that you may not have been cared for as a child or how a trauma affected your sense of safety or worthiness. I understand how scary that can be. I'm not asking you to uncover the exact reasons you're running (that will happen at a slow pace throughout the book). For now, just be brave enough to wonder. In order to let true healing begin, we must become conscious of our triggers and the feelings that live beneath our destructive patterns. A huge shift occurs when you become brave enough to look closely at what you've been unwilling to see. The key here is to go slowly.

The problem isn't that we're running, but that we are unwilling to face what we're running from and why.

No more time to hide

You might be thinking, *This feels too heavy; I should just skip ahead, or read one of her other books on manifesting.* I get it. It feels like hard work to face our past and heal. That's true, but it's much harder *not* to face it, stay stuck in the negative patterns, and never know true peace. But facing our truth is a spiritual practice and it's necessary in order to feel free. In fact, think twice before you skip ahead or pick up one of my manifesting books. This is my greatest manifestation because the more we heal, the happier we become, and the more joyful we are, the more we attract. Joy is the ultimate creator.

There is no more time to hide. When the stability of the world around us is shaken, we can become immobile and try to hide from our feelings. Or we can bust through and face the core wounds that made us run in the first place. At this moment, you have two choices: keep reading or shut the book and run.

If you keep reading, I can promise you emotional freedom on the other side. And with freedom comes joy. That's a *serious* promise and I wouldn't say it if I didn't mean it. If you decide to trust me and keep reading, I promise peace in the pages of this book. Trust that the journey I'm taking you on is safe and trust that you are spiritually guided. We will take it one step at a time.

Right now, let's keep it simple. I'm asking you to start by becoming brave enough to witness your triggers and the ways in which you run. This curiosity is necessary to establish a clear foundation through which you can take the next steps laid out before you—the steps to free yourself from childhood patterns that continue to play out in your life.

It's possible that you've never recognized your triggers or that you were running at all until reading this. Triggers are the moments when you feel most activated and possibly don't even know why. When triggered you can revert to childlike behavior or turn to a coping mechanism to numb out the uncomfortable feeling. A trigger happens when an event activates an implicit memory (emotional response) that brings forth an unresolved experience that you didn't like or couldn't control. Almost anything can serve as a trigger. A song can trigger an implicit memory of a time when you felt unsafe. Or a scent of cologne can trigger the feeling of being with someone who harmed you. In my case, it was a feeling of being out of control or taken advantage of. Without being aware of our triggers, we find ways to justify our behavior to make it acceptable. Maybe, like me, you say things to yourself like, "Everyone drinks a lot" or "It's totally normal to be stressed out all the time." Or maybe you haven't even tried to justify your behavior and have accepted destructive patterns as a part of who you are.

Identifying triggers

For now, we're not looking to uncover exactly *why* you're triggered to hide, run, or fight; instead, it's about looking at your patterns. I'll guide you through a writing practice of inquiry that is crucial on the path to freedom. We must be willing to look at what's up in order to show up for it. Do this practice when you have some free space for private, personal contemplation. It's valuable to do this practice in one sitting to allow the ability to get it all out onto the page. You may find that you want to return to this practice and add to it. That's fine.

If, for some reason, this practice feels too overwhelming and you can't even look at your triggers, that's okay too. Come back to it when you're ready. Maybe for now you simply need to read this book to take in the concepts. Then when you read it a second time, you'll do the practices. Go at your own pace. If you do go ahead with the exercise, it's possible that it may activate you. So make sure that after you write it all out you go for a walk, work out, or even dance around the room. Big personal growth work can make us feel immobile. The best antidote is to physically shake it out.

We must be willing to look at what's up in order to show up for it.

If you feel ready to begin, let's start by looking at the people, places, and situations in your life that trigger you to want to run, fight, turn to an addictive behavior, become overly reactive, or act out in some way. For example, it's common to be triggered in a romantic relationship when a partner reminds you of an unresolved implicit memory or experience you have of a parent or adult figure.

Let's look closely for those triggers.

Take out a journal and make three columns. In the first column, make a list of all of the ways you get triggered. Some of my personal triggers were (and I say *were* because they have subsided):

- When I was out of control at work

- Being told to shush

- Being taken advantage of

- Being told I was wrong

Be specific in your writing. For instance, maybe a trigger is when your husband leaves the house without saying goodbye. You don't need to figure out why it activates you so much; just write it down as something that triggers you. Be specific and don't edit a word. Let your pen flow without thinking. If you just write, you'll be amazed by what comes onto the page. Take a deep breath and begin this process.

After writing the list in column one, move on to column two, and make a new list of how each trigger makes you feel. For instance, whenever I was triggered by someone shushing me, I'd feel an insane rage brewing, as though I'd want to punch something. Be that specific. What feelings are activated when you're triggered? You may not be able to even recognize the feelings yet. Maybe all you notice is the desire to shut down or you become so overwhelmed that you go numb. That's totally normal. Just record whatever feelings (or lack thereof) come up for you when you're triggered.

Now move on to column three and record how you respond to your triggers and feelings. This is the column where you call out your reactions and responses—all the ways you hide, run, or fight. Here are some examples from my own life.

Trigger	Feeling	How I run from the feeling
Being out of control	I feel terrified. My stomach gets tight. My jaw clenches. Anxiety takes over.	I try to control other people and my surroundings. I overwork to the point of exhaustion in order to get back into a place of feeling in control.
When someone tells me to shush	I feel silently outraged and act defensive.	I push back on the other person, trying to figure out why they would shut me down.

You may find yourself leaving some columns blank. There is great freedom in this process even if you can't complete every box. Don't judge your process. Even if you fill out only one column, that's good. Be kind and gentle with yourself every step of the way. Don't overthink this or push yourself to go deeper. Honor yourself for having the bravery to even look at your responses.

Look at the patterns

If you're ready, now look for any patterns among the feelings that trigger your response to hide, run, or fight. Take note of the two most prominent feelings that arise when you're triggered. Was it anger and fear? Or judgment and defensiveness? Then take note of the two most common ways you run from those feelings, such as drinking, gossiping, overeating, shutting down, etc. You may even run from your triggers by going into a deep depression and catastrophizing.

For now, look at the surface feelings and immediate reactions. This practice is a powerful inquiry that will shine light on the patterns that have kept you living with a false sense of safety. Note that the feelings you have on the surface are real, but deeper feelings are underneath. Don't even try to face those deeper feelings yet. There's no need to rush.

Looking at surface feelings and immediate reactions is a powerful inquiry that will shine light on the patterns that have kept you living with a false sense of safety.

Please be kind to yourself. It can be painful to shine light on your triggers and the associated feelings and actions. That's why uninterrupted space to do the practice is so important. I highly recommend, however, that you don't do it before bed. Deep personal growth work before you go to sleep may interfere with your restful state. Instead, do this exercise at some point during the day that feels safe.

It takes a courageous person to notice their triggers. To have the willingness to take the next right action and look more closely at your patterns is a major accomplishment. This brave inquiry promises forward momentum. It's likely that you've spent your entire life avoiding and protecting yourself against these triggers, feelings, and reactions. That's the case for most people, even folks who've been committed to personal growth. Remember, I spent years in therapy performing for my shrink. For years, I pretended that everything was okay. It was only when I became brave enough to wonder why I was running that the next level of healing could set in.

It was only when I became brave
enough to wonder why I was running
that true healing started.

Breathe

A practice like this can bring up a lot of difficult and unwanted emotions. If you're overwhelmed, then use this moment as an opportunity to honor those feelings. To honor your feelings means to notice them, breathe into them, and accept them. Remember, the reason we run through negative and addictive habits is because we don't want to feel things from the past. When we honor our feelings, we can begin to relate to them in a new way, seeing ourselves (and all our big emotions) with compassion and acceptance.

1. Breathe in deeply, and allow yourself to be fully present with the feeling. One of the hardest habits to break is pushing away our negative feelings. Instead, give yourself the chance to become comfortable in the discomfort by breathing into them.

2. On the out breath, visualize your body releasing energy. You may even want to physically shake out your arms and legs to actively let go of tension in your body. The out breath offers freedom to release the tension and resistance.

3. Taking it further, wrap your arms around your body and give yourself a hug. Say to yourself, "I've got you. It's safe to move forward. You are not alone."

Let faith be part of this journey. Give yourself permission to breathe into the truth that you are supported and guided through every step of this journey. A spiritual presence of love will hold you and guide you, and so will I. I'm here for you on this path. I've laid out the steps toward peace and freedom in a way that is gentle. I will go slowly and keep you safe. Please know this: I care deeply about you, and I'm here for you all the way. We're in this together, my dear friend.

The feelings that make us most uncomfortable reveal to us what we need to heal.

Remember what I taught in Chapter 1: You're not alone in this inquiry. I spent over a decade running and suffering, but I never lost touch with the spiritual relationship that was guiding me every step of the way. That spiritual connection gave me faith even when fear overwhelmed me. Subconscious fears make us feel unsafe and alone; they are what made us run in the first place. But we can face those fears with spiritual guidance or love by our side. If you feel inspired, welcome a spiritual connection of your own understanding with this prayer:

Thank you, Universe (or your alternative word), for helping me feel safe and supported through this personal growth journey. I trust I'm being guided.

Prayers like this have kept me consistent in my healing journey. My unwavering faith in the Universe is what allowed me to bravely inquire about what lived beneath my patterns. I have always relied on Spirit to help me answer these questions and guide me. Today, when people ask me what I'm most proud of, my answer is simple: I'm proud of my courage to go to the places that scared me the most so that I could truly heal. Thanks to my spiritual relationship, I could handle some of the toughest circumstances with the faith that freedom and peace were on the other side.

While it may seem terrifying to look at your triggers and your responses, I can assure you freedom is always on the other side. The feelings that make us most uncomfortable reveal to us what we need to heal. Fearlessly looking at your triggers and defense mechanisms can feel empowering if you let it. Becoming aware of your behavior shines light on what you've been hiding. We cannot heal what we cannot see. You are taking a stand for change. You are committing to heal. Just reading this chapter is brave because it means you were willing to look more closely at yourself. Take that in. Your willingness begins the process of undoing the patterns you've set in. Become honest with yourself, and you become free.

CHAPTER 3

Why We Run

I was lying on the sofa in my therapist's office staring up at the ceiling. We'd discovered that I was more likely to open up when I wasn't looking at her. It felt less vulnerable. For the first time in over a decade of therapy, I started to talk about feelings I'd never shared. I told her that for my entire life I'd had a sense that I was being taken advantage of. Then out of nowhere, I said, "Even when I'm intimate."

Admitting this to her triggered something deep within me.

"AAAHHHHHHHHHHHH!" I screamed as I leaped off the sofa.

At that moment, I remembered.

A memory that had been hidden for more than 30 years. An exiled memory that had impacted every area of my life. The memory that I was running from: childhood sexual abuse.

This was one of the scariest moments of my life.

Remembering.

My body froze, my palms were sweaty, and my soul had leaped out of my body. The sounds in the room became so loud that I couldn't focus. I went numb. I felt as though I was thrown back into the trauma.

We had only a few more minutes left in our session. This was one of those moments when my therapist had to break the physical boundary between patient and provider and embrace me. She held me by the shoulders, looked me in the eye, and said, "I will call you as soon as I'm out of session. You are not alone in this. I am here." I walked out the door and got into the elevator. I couldn't make it down one floor without feeling extreme panic. So without thinking, I walked out of the elevator and took the stairs.

I walked out of the lobby and into the crowded New York City streets. Overwhelmed, I rushed into a clothing store a few doors over and straight into a dressing room. There I began to cry. Then I grabbed my phone to call my friend Elisa, who worked and specialized in trauma and addiction. I knew she could help.

"Elisa, I remembered being sexually abused as a child," I said.

She replied, "Gabby, I always suspected."

For a moment, I felt a sense of relief. *This is why I was a drug addict. This is why I'm a workaholic. This is why I'm terrified of true vulnerable connection.* The relief wore off fast though, and fear set in. I had to give a talk that night. Oh my God, how was I going to do it? I was scheduled to go onstage in an hour.

Pulling myself together, I headed over to the venue, where my husband greeted me. He noticed immediately that something was wrong. "Zach, I just remembered that I was sexually abused as a child." He looked at me with horror and confusion. Then he held me in his arms. More concerned about him, I said, "Don't worry, I'll get through this. I can get through this."

Then I stepped onto the stage. For that hour, my story was erased. For that hour, I could pretend like nothing happened. For that hour, I could hide from the reality of what I had remembered.

When I stepped off the stage, the reality of the memory set back in.

The moment I got home, I crawled under the covers and called my therapist. "You have recovered a dissociated memory," she said, and explained that I had been living in a state of dissociation because of a traumatic childhood event. Dissociation is a coping mechanism of disconnecting from the present moment so that one can get through a traumatic event without having to experience extreme emotions. It's as if you float above your body so you don't have to face the trauma. Often, traumatized people will continue to dissociate whenever the original trauma is triggered. When one dissociates, their mind can go blank, their eyes glaze over, they can feel numb, they disconnect from their surroundings and have an out-of-body experience.

While I had recalled the memory into my consciousness, I hadn't recovered all the details. I wasn't aware of exactly what happened or who abused me. And as much as I wanted to believe that it wasn't true, I'd never had such a strong sense of knowing in my life. I was absolutely sure that I had been abused.

Days later I scheduled a phone session with my therapist. On the call, I lay in my bed paralyzed by fear. I felt like a shell of myself. I explained to her that I'd been walking around totally unaware of my body, completely disconnected from life. I couldn't get into an elevator without having a panic attack. Whenever my husband tried to hug me, I went numb. She asked a series of questions.

"Have you uncovered any more memories?"

"No."

"Are you eating?"

"No."

She continued on to an exercise to help me get grounded in my body. She asked me to feel the bed underneath me. And then sense the floor underneath the bed. And the house holding up the floor. Then the earth beneath the house. As we finished the grounding exercise, I started to sense a new memory surfacing.

"AAAHHHHHHHHHHHHH!" I screamed. "I'm in the closet! I'm not alone! I'm not safe!"

In that moment, more fear set in as fragmented memories began to come together like a complicated puzzle. Images that I'd carried for years but couldn't understand now had meaning: Inside my childhood closet. The chest. The dollhouse. The small window looking out onto the driveway. The tiny door. These images had sifted in and out of my consciousness for decades, fragile pieces of a haunting memory.

The more details I recovered, the more real it became. This was the truth I'd been seeking, but now I wanted to give it all back. I was horrified to face the shameful truth that as a young innocent child I'd been sexually abused. While I couldn't uncover exactly what happened or who the abuser was, all of the physical symptoms and feelings that I'd experienced throughout my life pointed to abuse that was sexual in nature. I knew this because my body couldn't lie. I felt like there was a live wire of energy moving through me at all times. I could never be still and truly relax my body. Even in deep meditation, it felt like I had one eye open always on the lookout for danger.

A live wire of energy was moving through me at all times. Even in deep meditation, it felt like I had one eye open always on the lookout for danger.

Choosing survival

Now that the door to the closet had been opened, I could no longer hide (even though part of me desperately wanted to). Recovery was the only path I was willing to take. I had been brave enough to wonder, and now I had to become brave enough to survive with these memories. Not just survive but thrive as a result of my commitment to living free. Deep down I knew that my survival wasn't just for me. I knew in my heart that I would live to tell the story of true recovery so that others could begin to free themselves too.

The same way I dove into my sober recovery was how I approached my trauma healing. First, I built my team. I had weekly sessions with my therapist. Then I added weekly treatment with an Eye Movement Desensitization and Reprocessing (EMDR) specialist designed to heal the subconscious memories. In addition, I worked closely with an Emotional Freedom Techniques (EFT) coach who specialized in trauma recovery. (I will go into depth about these therapeutic treatments in later chapters and provide links to additional, free resources.) Even with all the therapeutic support that I was privileged enough to afford, I still had a long road ahead. I wanted to feel relief overnight, but that wasn't going to happen.

When I started to share my story with close friends in my sober recovery groups, they responded with, "Me too." I was blown away by the fact that so many women in sobriety had trauma stories. How was it that they had never shared about what was likely a major contributor to their addiction? Why was it so buried? Why in the most intimate recovery rooms did no one speak about sexual abuse? It was as if they'd tucked away the story in a box labeled "We Don't Go There."

I too had been unconsciously running from past trauma and was now terrified to face those repressed memories. When we push down our memories and unresolved traumas, we are never free from them. Instead, we relive them on a daily basis because they live in our body, our subconscious, and in all the ways we protect ourselves from feeling the repressed pain. Even though I wanted so badly to tuck it away and pretend it never happened, I was on a pursuit of freedom. I knew I had no other choice but to remain willing to face that resistance and show up for my trauma recovery.

When we push down our memories and unresolved traumas, we are never free from them. Instead, we relive them on a daily basis.

The effects of trauma

Unfortunately, the negative effects of trauma don't necessarily heal themselves. I once gave a talk for a group of 9/11 first responders. They shared about symptoms that plagued them nearly 10 years on. Symptoms ranging from dissociation (numbing out) to shock, rage, nervousness, terror, flashbacks, guilt, and addictive behaviors. These are all common responses to trauma, and they can get worse over time, damaging the nervous system, causing physical conditions, and negatively altering behavioral patterns. It was terribly sad to hear their stories, and I recognized myself in them. We shared a similar suffering. Their vulnerable accounts of their experiences helped me see how "normal" these emotional and physical responses are when one becomes traumatized.

For nearly 30 years, I lived with the silent belief that something was wrong with me. I believed that I was unable to live like a "normal" person. I found it so hard to deeply connect to people one on one. It was overwhelmingly difficult to focus in conversations with others. I felt disembodied and physically frozen. I had accepted that fate and believed that was just who I was. It was only when I started studying the neurobiology behind trauma and childhood stress that I could truly forgive myself for all the ways I'd been different. I could finally see that there was a reason for my suffering and that I wasn't alone in it. Awareness benefited me so much that I wanted to share with you a brief overview of what happens to the brain when one becomes traumatized. It's important to understand the mechanics as we work to reverse its negative effects.

When someone experiences a traumatic event, their amygdala (the emotional response center of the brain) often becomes overactive, which can lead to a heightened fear response, leaving the person in a persistent state of hyperarousal and stress. When faced with a traumatic event, the very parts of our brain that keep us safe can also be parts that lead us to live with a feeling of unsafety. Even though we can dissociate from the experience and seemingly forget that it happened, the brain still has the imprinted images and feelings associated with the trauma. Those do not disappear and can continue to affect us subconsciously. When a trauma is too painful to experience in the moment, or if we are powerless to fight or flee, we can dissociate and freeze, which impedes the trauma from being released from the body. When trauma cannot properly move through the nervous system from arousal all the way through to discharge, it becomes stuck not only in the body but also in the brain.

There it remains energetically present, leaving us in a constant state of alertness and on the lookout for danger.

When something seemingly threatening occurs, this sets off the amygdala's alarm system and sends the individual into a state of reliving the original trauma. *Small t* trauma and *big T* trauma both create a stress response. The difference is that the brain has the capacity to move a onetime *small t* trauma (such as a fender bender) through the nervous system and back to a baseline regulation. A *big T* trauma such as childhood traumatic events or ongoing neglect never fully complete the cycle back to baseline regulation. When a traumatic event is not fully processed or recalled, it can become more destructive than the original trauma itself, setting us into a constant state of hyperarousal.

Whenever I felt out of control at work, like if the website went down during a live webinar or a team member wasn't getting their job done, I would relive the feeling of being out of control as a child. I'd go into fight mode and fly off the handle, micromanage, and bring down the energy of the team. My brain couldn't differentiate between the minor work issue and the childhood trauma. This is hypervigilance, which means being on edge or aware of threat at all times. I lived in a state of hypervigilance for 30 years. No wonder I turned to drugs, alcohol, and work addiction to numb out from this constant state of arousal.

My greater awareness of the neurological and physiological effects of trauma helped me understand decades of my behavior. I could see clearly how some of my darkest behavioral patterns were not my fault or my choice. They were the result of a compromised nervous system and the effects the trauma had on my brain. Instead of thinking something was wrong with me, I could witness myself through the lens of love, acceptance, and compassion. Seeing myself in this new way was a huge relief and offered me the opportunity to go deeper in my healing.

Trauma and memory

The brain has a number of ways to deal with traumatic events, including trying to help you forget about them. In the case of someone who cannot fight or flee, they become frozen. The freeze response sends the body into a state of immobility, releasing chemicals that numb the body or mind. The brain shuts off and disconnects from the present moment. This is known as dissociation and is a common trauma response. In cases of *big T* trauma, a memory can be "forgotten" for decades only to be revealed through a trigger or when someone becomes safe enough to recall the memory. It's also common for people not to remember events right before or right after they occur. A trauma victim may only have access to fragmented pieces of the experience. These fragmented memories can feel like flashbacks or images on a movie screen that pop into consciousness at random. In my case, I always had a visual memory of the closet, the dollhouse, and the window.

While dissociation can initially be a protective mechanism, it can also become a source of harm to one's emotional and physical well-being. Even though a memory may be "lost," it's still alive in the subconscious and can elicit emotions and reactions. The smallest things can trigger implicit unconscious memories of an experience, sending one into a state of fight, flight, or freeze. A traumatized person doesn't necessarily have a frame of reference for why they feel reactive in that way. I remember saying to my therapist, "Wouldn't it have just been easier if I hadn't remembered my trauma?" She responded, "Your body remembers it every day of your life." In reality we can't run from a dissociated memory.

Traumatized people may continuously
relive the experience of the past as
if it's happening in the present with no
cognitive understanding of what's going on.

It was helpful for me to understand the physiology behind why and how my body tried to keep me safe from overwhelming and terrifying childhood experiences. My brain's ability to send me into freeze mode during the abuse is what allowed me to dissociate in the moment. The emotions would have been far too overwhelming for me at such a young age. But the memories never left my subconscious, and consequently I could never really find a place of safety.

In retrospect I can see how I spent every moment trying to feel safe. Unresolved trauma symptoms haunted my waking moments and my sleep. At night, I'd be on high alert. My jaw would clench, my body would stiffen, and I'd even wake up with pain in my wrists from sleeping with my hands in a fist.

In addition, it affected the way I related to everyone around me. It kept me from being able to truly connect and trust others. Trauma was the reason for my core fear of being alone and unsafe while simultaneously preventing me from truly connecting with others. It also caused me to suffer from many physical conditions previously mentioned—gastrointestinal issues, insomnia, back pain, TMJ, and so much more.

Spirit kept me safe

My therapist helped me understand why it took me 30 years to become safe enough to remember the trauma. All the work we'd done together, my sober recovery, my yoga/meditation training, my devoted spiritual practice, and my commitment to serve, helped me get to a place where I was safe enough to remember what happened in my childhood. My spiritual connection kept me sober and committed to healing. I can see clearly now how there was a spiritual force of love behind every step toward remembering and every healing step beyond that day.

Spirit is guiding you too, right here, right now. When I started speaking publicly about my traumatic memory, people began to tell me how hearing my story came at the exact moment they needed to accept their own. I know that Spirit guided them to me at the exact right moment in time to take the next step forward in their life. Whether they heard me share on a podcast or at a workshop, they were guided to hear my story so that they could accept their own. This may be the case for you. Don't underestimate the spiritual presence that led you to this book. Spirit will guide you to the exact books, teachers, and support you need. I believe you were guided here. Maybe you recognize yourself in me, or can finally see how your suffering is far more common than you thought. The more I learned about the effects of trauma, the more "textbook" I felt. This was actually helpful. I was grateful to be able to normalize my experience and feel less alone in my suffering. I hope I can do the same for you no matter how big or small your experiences have been.

I went into this writing process willing to reveal it all, in an effort to help you know that you are not alone. I made this commitment because I knew it was my responsibility to share my truth in the pursuit of service and love. I found great reprieve in hearing other people's stories because they gave me a sense of spiritual connection and I felt less alone. That is my hope for you too.

The greatest support system of all is your spiritual connection. Let's take a moment now to invite Spirit into this process. If you're feeling activated or triggered in any way you can always seek support through prayer. At any moment that you feel afraid to move forward, you can pray for relief. A simple prayer such as "Thank you, Spirit, for guiding my path" is enough to feel peace wash over you.

Prayer allows you to give over any fear that comes up and welcome intuitive guidance to show you where to go and what to do to feel safe in your mind and body. Throughout your journey with this book, return to prayer, over and over again. When we pray, we temporarily suspend our fears and open up our consciousness to receive intuitive guidance. Prayer will open you up to the exact therapist who can support you, or the intuition to follow one of my suggested methods, and it will help you release your fears on a moment-to-moment basis. I hope you feel safe knowing that Spirit is leading your path.

Take your time with this content, and trust your own pace. In an effort to support you, I've included practices that you can apply immediately to get relief. It's also important to note that my story can be very triggering to anyone who has unresolved trauma. If reading this is activating you and it feels too scary to face, I highly recommend that you seek therapeutic counsel. Facing unresolved trauma (*small t* or *big T*) can be terrifying and requires a support system. I have compiled a detailed resource list of therapists who specialize in these issues. Visit DearGabby.com/HappyResources if you need additional support.

Thank you, Spirit, for guiding
me to what I know to be true.

You no longer have to run

Whether or not you're aware of the traumatic events in your life, they have impacted you. Many people blow off the fearful events from their past saying, "Oh, I addressed that when I was fifteen" or "That was so many years ago; it doesn't matter now." But the unresolved disruptive moments from your past are exactly what you're running from or fighting here in the present. In my personal friendships and in my work, I am a frequent witness to people hiding from the true reasons behind their suffering. Just today, a close friend revealed to me that a social media post triggered an unresolved experience from her childhood.

"I'm so afraid to say something wrong or get negative comments. I don't want anyone not to like me," she kept saying.

"Does this feeling seem familiar to you?" I asked.

And after a little digging, she responded, "Well, when I was 13, I had an abusive boyfriend. He constantly made me feel like I wasn't good enough, and I'd do anything to make him like me. But that was so long ago. And I finally broke up with him so I'm sure I resolved it. But maybe not."

At that moment, she realized that the 13-year-old girl who was traumatized by her boyfriend was still showing up in her relationships years later. This explained why she always complained of trying to be a "good girl" in order to be liked at work and with friends. Playing small and hiding out are ways she's been running from unresolved feelings of inadequacy. While my friend had done a ton of spiritual and personal growth work, deep down she was still terrified and hadn't faced the subconscious reason she was running.

Awareness is the catalyst for recovery. Respect and honor all of your experiences and be compassionate toward yourself. You've been doing your best to keep yourself safe and now, with greater awareness, you can move toward true safety. Noticing your wounds is the first step to healing them.

We all have past experiences that shape the course of our lives. Some people have had trauma with a *big T*, like in the case of child abuse, sexual assault, near-death experiences, etc. And most all of us have experienced trauma with a *small t*, such as being told we're stupid, being bullied on the playground, or even living through a worldwide pandemic. We're trying to get through each day, but our amygdala is continuously interrupting with the fight, flight, or freeze response. Even for well-adjusted adults, everything from online comments to a trip to the grocery store with a mask can feel like a threat.

You may have found yourself running from the trauma of 2020 in chaotic ways. Maybe you've become agoraphobic. Maybe you're seeing symptoms of OCD (obsessive-compulsive disorder) spike, or maybe you've found yourself addicted to sleep medication. This may reveal a pattern and point to a past fearful event. Give yourself permission to acknowledge those fearful experiences and honor yourself and all that you've been through. The processes in this book will help you release them from your subconscious so you can transform your behaviors and reactivity. No matter how big or small the trauma may have been, recovery is ahead, and you can stop running from the past. We are all innocent children who have faced terrifying experiences, but running or fighting only keeps us in a state of perpetual fear. When we become brave enough to look at the ways we've been running and fighting, we then can start true healing.

Fear is why we run

Upon remembering my childhood trauma, I was able to face the truth behind why I ran. I could see clearly why I'd become a drug addict and alcoholic. I understood my workaholism, codependency, and inability to be vulnerable and present in my close relationships. I could see how running seemed like the only option because my brain and body had never processed the fear from the trauma that I experienced as a young child. While I'd been aware of my destructive behavior before 2016, I was unaware of *why* it was there. Remembering the trauma gave me a clear understanding of why I behaved as I did. But most important, it gave me great compassion for myself—a compassion that would carry me further into the long-lasting recovery I longed for.

We are born with faith in love, but the moment we experience the fears of the world, we lose sight of that love, and then fear, judgment, and separation become our defense. Fear runs the show, and the voice of love becomes a distant afterthought. Fear is the emotion below the other impermissible feelings of being inadequate, unlovable, unworthy, unsafe, etc. These emotions are so terrifying that any time the past fearful experience is triggered, we will do something to run from or fight it. We'll drink, work, avoid, judge, anything not to have to relive that suffering. But running from our suffering keeps it alive. We become like a hamster in a wheel running from ourselves. We think we're running away from pain, but we're not going anywhere. We remain stuck in a cycle of fear.

It's common to rely so much on our coping mechanisms that we falsely believe we won't survive without them. When I started to heal my patterns, I noticed that a part of me was afraid to let them go. I was worried that if I let go of the work addiction, I'd lose my ability to write books, grow my business, get it all done. I'd measured so much of my success on how hard I worked. What I learned, though, is that the more grounded and healed my inner world was, the more impactful I could be in every area of life. I didn't lose my edge; I softened my edges.

Maybe you're afraid of leaving the relationship that isn't serving you because you'll feel inadequate without a partner. Or maybe you're afraid that if you stop drinking you won't be cool in social situations. I understand why you'd be afraid to face your fear and give up your coping mechanisms. After all, you built up these habits as a defense against fear. Why would you ever lay them down? The answer is because you want to feel better, you want to feel free. The metaphysical text *A Course in Miracles* says, "In my defenselessness my safety lies."[1] As scary as this may sound, you'll have to take my word for it for now. The moment you lay down your defenses against fear, love can reemerge. I'm not suggesting you give up your defense mechanisms overnight. That would be too scary. But for now, become conscious of them. Start to pay attention to the ways you run. All the ways you defend against fear have been helpful in that they have kept you temporarily safe from the overwhelming feelings that live beneath them. But that's not sustainable. By heightening awareness of the ways you run from fear, you slow down enough to get closer to your truth. Freedom from fear offers you the freedom to be the greatest version of yourself.

The moment you lay down your defenses against fear, love can reemerge.

Interrupt the fear response

Establishing a sense of safety and relief begins by interrupting the fear response. The following practice is designed to create an interruption in your patterns and all the ways you run from fear. If you begin to notice your fear and choose instead to interrupt it, then you don't need to run. Even if you are not aware of what you're running from, this process will still help in the undoing of destructive patterns and avoidance tactics. In the 12 steps of Alcoholics Anonymous (AA), if you feel the urge to drink, you call your sponsor or go to a meeting. In my early sobriety, this kept me sober. Each time I noticed myself wanting to pick up a drink (my response to fear), I'd call my sponsor or go to a meeting. By interrupting the old pattern with a call or a meeting, I could create a new, healthy pattern.

Noticing your reactive response is a huge step in changing the pattern. In this context, the reactive states of shaming, blaming, yelling, and avoiding are the same as drinking, overeating, or overworking. Anything we do to avoid an impermissible feeling is a form of running from an impermissible feeling.

The moment you enter into a reactive state, pause or take a time-out, then follow the steps below.

1. Review your triggers and the way you run (from Chapter 2).

In Chapter 2 you took a close look at the ways your feelings triggered an emotional response. With this newfound awareness, ask yourself: *Can I identify fear underneath those responses?*

2. Pay attention to the moments that you want to run.

Throughout the day, pay attention to your feelings and the moments when you are triggered into one of your destructive patterns. At times you may not notice you were running until after the fact. That's totally fine; this practice is about awareness. The more awareness you bring to your feelings and behaviors, the easier it will be to catch yourself in the act.

3. Interrupt the reactive response by journaling.

Answer the following questions in your journal:

- What am I feeling right now? *Describe your feelings.*

- What could be triggering this feeling? *Describe the situation.*

- What do I want to do to fight this feeling? *Describe in detail.*

- What can I do instead? *List out healthy ways that you could respond to these feelings, such as call a friend and vent, go for a walk, cry, write about it in your journal, stretch your body, say a prayer, sit in meditation, or even schedule an appointment with your therapist. The way to begin the process of undoing negative reactivity is to put something productive, spiritual, and grounding in place of your reactive response. Each time you do this, you will create a new neural pathway in your brain.*

4. Breathe.

If you're struggling to figure out what to do instead of reacting, revisit the breath practice from Chapter 2 (as seen below). This practice of connecting to your breath interrupts the pattern of running and avoiding your feelings. Instead of running, practice breathing.

- Breathe in through your mouth for two seconds, breathing into the feelings of discomfort.
- Hold your breath in for two seconds.
- Exhale for two seconds, releasing all feelings of discomfort.
- Hold your breath out for two seconds.
- Repeat at least 10 times.

5. Pray.

Another grounding way to interrupt your pattern is to say a prayer. *A Course in Miracles* says, "Prayer is the medium of miracles."[2] From the *Course* perspective, a miracle is a shift in perception. When you pray, you offer up your ego's story (fear of the past, present, and future) and welcome a new perspective. When you pray, you'll feel great relief in the belief that you're giving over your will and allowing the Universe, God, love (or whatever you call it) to take the lead. Here's a prayer to say when you notice yourself triggered in a reactive response:

Thank you, Universe, for helping me experience these feelings with grace. I honor how I feel.

This prayer has the power to instantly shift your perception from focusing on fear to spiritual, loving solutions instead.

Choose one of the suggestions for interrupting your reactive response and start practicing it. Don't overthink it; just do it.

Take a step forward

Here's an example of how these practices helped a close friend of mine. My friend's pattern of running came in the form of shaming and blaming other people for her discomfort. When she identified triggers and responses in Chapter 2, this is what she came up with:

Trigger	Feeling	How you run from the feeling
Not having my feelings and needs met	I feel outraged, angry, and like I want to fight.	I shut down, show everyone around me that I'm upset, and in some way blame someone else. I shame and blame others (especially my husband).

This pattern of shaming and blaming was destructive to her relationships. Her marriage suffered, her friendships were difficult, and worst of all she never felt like she was getting what she wanted. Shaming and blaming was just a form of running from a deep-rooted pain. And while she wasn't ready to face that pain, she was willing to interrupt the reactive pattern for the sake of her marriage. So each time she could sense the anger rising, she'd breathe, take a few moments to pause, or even excuse herself to go to the bathroom instead of defaulting to shame and blame. Doing so allowed her to come back to the situation (and her husband) with a heart-centered response. Instead of acting out, she could express her feelings and needs in a calm and neutral tone, saying something like, "I feel upset when you interrupt me." The tone with which she'd respond then no longer triggered his wounds and fear. This was a leap forward in undoing a pattern she'd lived with for a lifetime and created more peace in her relationships.

All I'm asking you to do is pay attention to your patterns and start to interrupt them. If you're not ready to look back at your past for the roots of your triggers and responses, that's okay. It's important to take this work slowly and be gentle with yourself. Go at your own pace. Applying this practice will benefit you in deep ways. You may notice that people around you feel more connected and safe in your presence. You'll begin to release a victim mentality and recognize and interrupt your triggers more quickly. You may even start to discover something from your past that is ready to come to the surface. Honoring your triggers and being willing to contemplate a new perspective is brave. My hope is that these steps become second nature for you.

Notice what works

Now you have a practice to unwind your reactivity so you can become more conscious of your feelings in the moment. Let this practice of noticing and interrupting your patterns be a step forward in preparing you to do the deeper work of healing the reasons why you ran in the first place. Start building up an arsenal of tools that can replace your trigger responses. Dissolve your fear-based patterns with love.

You've already begun to do deep and transformational work. By looking at your patterns, triggers, and wounds, you're facing feelings you may have never noticed. You're putting a new pattern in place of your reactivity and taking ownership of your life. Big work, my friend. It's huge! With this new perception of your life, you will be tempted at times to retreat and run from the big feelings that may come up. That's to be expected. Notice when you fall into an old pattern of running from fear, forgive yourself, and return to the prayers and practices above. Remember that you are not alone. Each time you turn to prayer, breath, or any loving practice, the love of the Universe can take over and put you right back on the path toward peace.

Trust what is true for you

By now you may come to recognize feelings of anxiety, fear, and inadequacy that have been with you since childhood. You may have done a lot of personal growth work and be aware of the stories behind these feelings. Or maybe you're just beginning to think about what's in your past. Either way, when you first begin to face the feelings behind the ways you run or avoid, it can be overwhelming, to say the least. Facing what happened to you as a child (and throughout your life) is painful. And the voice of fear will do everything in its power to convince you not to look at your suffering. It may even convince you that the suffering isn't real. In the case of trauma, sometimes it feels too shameful to admit what has happened. (We'll cover shame in the forthcoming chapters.)

The months after I remembered my childhood trauma were so scary that I sometimes tried to pretend like it didn't happen. I would question my memories and pray that they weren't true. I was paralyzed by the possibility that this could be my story. In those moments, I sought spiritual guidance.

Throughout my life I'd learned to rely on the guidance of a spiritual presence to help me whenever I felt blocked. No matter how difficult things could be, I believed that I was always being guided. So instead of shaming myself for having the memories, I asked for a sign that I was on the right track toward recovery. I've often found that one of the greatest ways to receive spiritual guidance is to ask for a clear message and sign (something that wouldn't be easy or obvious). I prayed, "Show me a blue butterfly to confirm that I'm on the right healing path." Then I surrendered it over to the care of my Higher Power to reveal the truth to me.

The following morning, my husband and I got in the car to drive to my in-laws. In the car, we were listening to a podcast and I was trying to get my mind off of the depressed feelings and thoughts that had been plaguing me. We turned the corner and stopped at a red light. I looked up and right in front of me was a jeep with a spare tire attached to the back. The tire had a cover on it with nearly twenty stickers of blue butterflies. Tears rolled down my cheeks and my heart filled with gratitude. In my darkest moment Spirit was there to remind me that I wasn't alone.

Invite Spirit into your healing journey

I've asked you to unpack the deepest feelings beneath your triggers and reactions. You're brave. It's no small thing to look at and accept the ways you run from fear. When you're facing difficult patterns and experiences from your past, you can feel really alone. In moments of deep suffering, it's hard to remember that we all suffer. You may think you're the only person on the planet struggling in this way. That's why tuning in to Spirit has given me strength, knowing that I am not alone on the journey. I have grown to rely on the intuitive voice of wisdom and the direction from the Universe. Every step of my healing path has been guided in the most magnificent way. I welcome you to invite Spirit into your healing journey now. Even if spirituality is new to you, this journey can be an opportunity to connect to an inner guidance you've never known. Sometimes it's the darkest moments that offer us the deepest spiritual connection.

Sometimes it's the darkest moments that offer us the deepest spiritual connection.

You have already begun to receive guidance. You wouldn't be reading this book right now if you hadn't been open to receiving intuitive spiritual guidance. You were guided to it. An inner call said, "Yes, I'm ready for that." So let's strengthen that inner voice and give you a sense of safety that you are supported every step of the way.

Whenever you're in doubt, whenever you feel lost, and whenever fear tries to stop you from moving forward with your growth, turn to prayer—even if you don't yet identify as a spiritual person or have a connection to God, the Universe, or Spirit. For the sake of this prayer, let's use the universal word *love*. The love within us and around us is an ever-present force guiding our journey. When we surrender to that love, we open up our consciousness to receive miraculous guidance and wisdom.

I'm willing to witness my fear and surrender to love.

By saying this prayer, you open your mind to receive the exact guidance, direction, and inspiration you need to move forward with confidence and faith. Whenever you feel stuck or afraid, return to this prayer. Doing this type of deep personal growth work requires a spiritual surrender. It's the spiritual surrender that allows you to get out of the way and let miracles unfold.

In retrospect, I can see how my spiritual faith gave me the bravery and foundation to face my unresolved traumatic memories. I had to become brave enough to wonder why I was running and let the truth be revealed. Even when I thought the truth would destroy me, it ultimately became what set me free.

CHAPTER 4

Hiding behind the Body

"With every breath I take, I am sending love, gratitude and healing to every single cell in my body. Yes, yes, yes, yes." These are the words of my late friend and publisher, Louise Hay. Lulu (as we call her over at Hay House) was a pioneer in mind-body healing. She brought transformational metaphysical principles to the world through her book *You Can Heal Your Life*. The premise of the book was that our physical symptoms are directly connected to our thoughts and beliefs. Underneath physical "dis-ease" is a root-cause emotional condition that needs to be processed. According to Louise, "If we are willing to do the mental work, almost anything can be healed."

I always held this belief system as truth, but it took years for me to apply it. Throughout my life, I had suffered with gastrointestinal issues. And after remembering the trauma of my childhood, my gut really flared up. I began having severe acid reflux, heartburn, and esophageal pain to the point that I struggled to breathe. This was in spite of my excellent diet, exercise routine, and overall healthy lifestyle. After a series of doctors' appointments and an upper endoscopy, the results revealed that I had severe gastritis, which is inflammation of the stomach lining typically due to poor diet or stress. With medicine and a specific diet, I was able to get my stomach back to baseline. But I continued to have regular flare-ups. According to my doctor, "This will just be something you'll have to deal with for the rest of your life." I was unwilling to accept this diagnosis.

Fortunately, I was guided to a naturopath in California who gave me a clear direction on how to cure my gastrointestinal condition. This was no small feat. For more than six months, I cooked every single meal myself and kept an extremely strict diet. Most important, I had to assume a zero stress tolerance. Stress was no longer an option. When you're stressed, your gut motility (aka the stretching and contractions of the muscles in your gastrointestinal tract) slows down, causing myriad gastrointestinal issues.

This six-month period proved deeply healing mainly because I had finally made the commitment to lower my stress levels. That was the first step to recognizing how much stress had affected my physical health. I came to accept that the inflammation in my gut was directly affected by my inflamed thoughts, unresolved emotions, and all the reactive ways I responded to my triggers. It was now time to heal the underlying root-cause beliefs that kept me reverting back into stress and fear.

While I was only two years into the trauma recovery, I was conscious enough to realize that the gut issues were not because of food or bacteria. In fact, I didn't have a gut problem; I had a subconscious emotional problem. Taking the time to be still and reflect on my life, I became very aware of all the ways that living the unresolved feelings and fearful beliefs had affected my body. Through my continued inner exploration, I could clearly see how my other physical symptoms— severe TMJ, chronic pain in my hips, and sciatica—were also the result of unresolved emotional distress.

I came to accept that I didn't have a gut problem;
I still had a subconscious emotional problem.

Additionally, I was still having two or three therapy sessions a week where I practiced EMDR (Eye Movement Desensitization and Reprocessing) and EFT (Emotional Freedom Techniques). Both practices stimulate different parts of the brain to encourage processing and healing of deeper wounds in order to clear out the energetic disturbances. While they work differently, both are intended to expand one's ability to tolerate unresolved emotions. These practices were cathartic and helped my body relax so my nervous system could regulate. I told my team that I had no choice but to step back from work and heal. In the six months that I spent releasing stress-related gastro issues, I felt more physically free. I slept well, my energy was high, my skin was clear, and I was the least stressed and triggered I'd ever been. I began to experience firsthand the direct correlation between my mind and my body. This was no longer something I understood intellectually; it became something I knew to be true.

The mind-body connection

With the desire to learn more about the mind-body connection, I began to study the work of Dr. John Sarno, the author of *Healing Back Pain* and *The Mindbody Prescription* (and several other life-changing books). Dr. Sarno worked as a professor of rehabilitation medicine at New York University School of Medicine and as director of the outpatient department at the Rusk Institute. Over the years of treating pain through physical therapy and medicine, he struggled with a harsh reality: Lots of people were not getting better. As a result, he developed a thesis that he referred to as TMS, tension myoneural syndrome (not currently accepted in mainstream medicine), which attributes many types of pain as a psychosomatic condition (a physical condition caused by inner conflict or stress).[1]

The core principle behind Dr. Sarno's work, much like that of Louise Hay, is the philosophy that physical pain derives from impermissible rage, fear, and unresolved emotional distress. Dr. Sarno believed that the brain would use physical pain as a way to distract us from otherwise facing our deep-rooted unconscious emotions. This would happen on a subconscious level. It's as though the brain uses the body as a coping mechanism, and just like our other coping mechanisms, physical problems become a form of distraction from true underlying healing. (Note that Dr. Sarno would always encourage patients to also seek medical care and treatment.)

Applying Dr. Sarno's theory requires that the patient be open to seeing the pain as a psychosomatic condition rather than only a physical diagnosis. This concept can be jarring for anyone who's suffering from chronic pain. You may be reading this right now thinking, *My physical pain is because of a herniated disk and has nothing to do with my emotions.* Or you may be thinking, *What is she talking about?! I have a diagnosis of IBS, and I've never had a healthy gut.* Dr. Sarno believed that the physical diagnosis is actually contributing to the problem. Once we are diagnosed with IBS (irritable bowel syndrome), a herniated disk, fibromyalgia, or other syndromes, we use the diagnosis as another way of avoiding the deep-rooted emotional conditions that live beneath our suffering.

A close friend suffered from constant back pain—really serious pain that kept him from participating in normal life. He often attributed it to a herniated disk. From my vantage point, however, I could see pretty clearly that his back would go out at the exact moment of a big life change or major emotional stressor. For instance, right after making a big career change, almost the next day, he struggled to even walk. He literally spent hours of each day, for weeks on end, lying on the floor. The pain made sleep impossible, and he would get just a few hours a night.

You cannot force the Sarno perception of a psychosomatic condition onto anyone—especially someone who suffers from chronic pain. And yet, as the years went on and my friend's pain persisted, he became more willing to try out alternatives. He would have moments of living pain-free and days of real suffering. The seemingly randomness of it made him believe that perhaps there was a spiritual solution. Once, while he was on vacation, he called me from bed in the middle of the day. The pain had come on out of the blue, he said. The day before he was swimming and hiking and today he was afraid that he might not be able to get to the airport to get home. So, he was in a bad place. "What's been going on? How was vacation before this?" I asked. "Oh, great. Yeah, weather, family, all good," he said. "Oh, and I just signed a contract on an apartment." And had I not been on the phone with him, I might not have believed what happened next. Simply by saying out loud the fear of a big financial commitment, he was able to give voice to his acute stress and anxiety. As if by magic, his brain stopped attacking his body. The underlying, emotional issue became obvious. And like the job before, the stress associated with a big financial decision left unchecked found its way to his back. But once he shined the light on the stress, the pain lifted just as quickly as it arrived. Healing the emotional stressors let his body off the hook.

Sympathetic overdrive

The times in my life when my gut was the most inflamed were when I was the most triggered by emotional upheaval. The months following the recall of my trauma were the scariest. I was terrified of what I'd remembered, and I wanted nothing more than to suppress the feelings and memories. That's when my brain distracted me from feeling the real emotions by projecting the pain onto my stomach.

When past traumatic events are unresolved emotionally, the body takes the heat. The body is constantly bombarded with the brain's stress responses. When someone has good digestion, a relaxed body, and minimal tension, they're living in the parasympathetic state. This is a calm state in which your energy is conserved, you're relaxed, your heart rate slows down, and your digestive tract is working properly.

When past traumatic events are unresolved emotionally, the body takes the heat.

The opposite of the parasympathetic state is known as sympathetic arousal. When your sympathetic nervous system is activated, your stomach tightens, the motility of the GI system is inhibited, and digestion slows down (in addition to other physical symptoms of inflammation and pain). Energy is cut off for metabolic digestion because the body allocates resources toward your heart and muscles, increasing blood pressure, heart rate, and respiration to fight or flee. Our brain says, "I have to prepare to fight." So it takes away energy from motility to put energy into reactivity. Your muscles become tense to prepare for the perceived threat. The brain focuses energy toward escaping that threat. This automatic response is beneficial if you're addressing a real, physical emergency, but it's detrimental when facing historical trauma.

When you're unaware of your emotional disturbances or unwilling to face past trauma, you can get stuck in sympathetic overdrive. A chronic state of hyperarousal taxes the vagus nerve (meant to regulate the parasympathetic nervous system).[2] When you get into this state, your heart rate can drop, you can become faint, and the muscles in your gut contract, leading to symptoms such as diarrhea, bloating, cramps, stomach spasms, and other forms of gut dysbiosis. Other physical symptoms include:

- Anxiety
- Panic attacks
- Nervousness
- Insomnia
- Breathlessness
- Palpitations
- Inability to relax or focus
- Jitters
- Gastrointestinal issues
- Intense fear
- Physical pain, and more

My gastrointestinal issues were the direct reflection of chronic hyperarousal. The parts of my brain that are designed to monitor danger remained overactivated for decades. Even the slightest sense of "danger," such as thinking someone was taking advantage of me or feeling out of control at work, could trigger an acute stress response. I would then go into an intense state of emotional distress, so my brain limited oxygen to my gut creating inflammation, slowing down the gastric motility, and even negatively affecting my microbiome. The stress also led to clenching my jaw, tension in my neck, and chronic pain in my hip. Because the balance was never restored, I lived with persistent distress throughout my body. My focus became all about healing my body, masking the feelings of rage, shame, and grief, which I hadn't yet discovered or addressed.

Body identification

Dr. Sarno's theory mirrors many spiritual philosophies about the body.

One of the most valuable messages from the metaphysical text *A Course in Miracles* is Lesson 199, "I am not a body. I am free." The text explains, "Freedom must be impossible as long as you perceive a body as yourself."[3] To me, this means that if we decide to perceive our physical experience as a reflection of our thoughts and feelings, we welcome a spiritual shift. Taking the focus off of the body and back onto healing the mind is a profound spiritual adjustment. I'm not suggesting we ignore our physical symptoms or fail to seek medical guidance, but that we simultaneously address the metaphysical effects of our mind. How different would we be if we were to dissolve our "body identification" and surrender to our inner awareness? When we tend to our spirit, we set our body free.

By focusing my energy inward through spiritual practice and personal development, my perception of my body has changed. The more I focus on freedom from fear, the more free I become from my bodily perceptions. It's not that I walk around all day ignoring or denying my body, it's just that I don't hide behind it as a way of running from my unresolved emotions. I turn to my spiritual development to heal the fears I've built up over the years. And reprogramming my thoughts from fear to love allows my body to respond accordingly. I recognize now all the ways my body can let me know when my inner world needs help and healing.

A spiritual relationship to your body

My newfound faith in the mind-body connection helped me see my body as a learning device to get closer to inner freedom. These days I am consciously aware of how my body responds to stressors, fearful thoughts, triggers, and feelings. Instead of being distracted by my body and physical pain and ignoring my inner emotional landscape, I can now take my body's cues as direction to turn inward and look for emotional disturbances that need tending to. Today, I can respectfully honor my body for all of its hard work and for taking the brunt of suffering in trying to protect me from impermissible feelings.

Several practices in particular really helped me establish a spiritual relationship with my body. These practices proactively soothed my nervous system, calmed my mind, and addressed the thoughts and feelings behind my body's response in the moment. This began my journey of undoing my fear of my body and reclaiming the spiritual presence of peace within me.

As I share these practices with you, you may not be able to contemplate a world without physical pain or a chronic illness. Once you identify your fears, your stress, or a trauma, don't expect your body to be released from tension instantly (although Dr. Sarno thought that was possible, and it was for the friend I mentioned earlier in the chapter). All I ask is that you open up to the possibility that your physical issues could have a mental or emotional component. We can open up your conscious awareness of your emotional connection to your body through prayer. Take a moment to say this prayer out loud and welcome Spirit into the process:

With love and compassion, I witness my physical suffering. Thank you, Spirit, for helping me resolve all emotional distress so my body can be restored back to peace.

Shine light on stress

What I loved most about Sarno and his approach to physical healing was how spiritual it was. I could see clearly how my stomach would flare up every time I went into a panic or defensive state. I was able to identify how each thought I had affected my beliefs and, therefore, my body. My conscious awareness of how my thoughts affected my body began a new relationship to my physical well-being. I committed to heal by addressing the root cause of the stress that was wreaking havoc in my body.

When we shine light on the thoughts rather than the physical symptoms, the symptoms can subside. What we focus on we create more of. Therefore, if we redirect our focus off our body and onto shifting our perception, we can experience great relief. The first step to healing the body is to shine light on the mind-body connection.

Take note of the ways your body responds to stress, fear, and overwhelming emotions. Do you have back pain? Migraines? Do you suffer from insomnia or dermatological issues? Have you been diagnosed with IBS or another gastrointestinal disorder? Do you have a diagnosis like fibro-myalgia or another inflammatory condition? Now consider the ways your thoughts and emotional condition may affect your physical condition. When you're really stressed, do your symptoms increase? Or when you experience one of the triggers we outlined in Chapter 2, do you notice your symptoms flare up? It may be hard to track in this moment how your body responds to stressors, but the next time you notice that back pain, or migraine, or stomach flare-up, ask yourself, "What am I thinking?" or "What emotion is behind this right now?" This simple inquiry will begin the process of helping you track your own mind-body connection. Instead of pushing past the pain or addressing it only from an allopathic approach, consider the emotional distur-bances that could lie beneath it. There is no shame in taking medicine or seeing a doctor, but give your body the chance to speak to you. Your physical pain is a clue that there is emotional pain that must be addressed.

Talk back to your brain

Your willingness to consider that your thoughts and emotions are affecting your body is a step toward undo-ing chronic physical conditions and setting your body free. Bringing attention to the mind-body connection gives voice to the unconscious emotions that deserve to be brought to the surface for healing. Remember that Dr. Sarno taught that the brain creates physical symptoms as a way to distract us from unconscious negative emotions. One of the key steps in Dr. Sarno's method is to repudiate the pain. By literally talking back to your brain and saying something like, "You are not my pain. I'm just avoiding a repressed emotion," you send a message to your brain to interrupt its process in order to protect you. In less severe cases of repressed emotions, simply repudiating the pain is enough to instantly stop it. Awareness that the symptom is created initially in the brain rather than the body stops the protective mechanism and the symptoms can subside.

In the previous chapters you've begun to identify the emotions that you've been running from or fighting. The work you've done thus far has brought a heightened level of awareness to the emotional distress in your life and where fear may be an underlying emotion. Now let's take a closer look. While you may not yet absolve yourself of emotional distress, you can give it a voice.

It's brave to allow subconscious emotions like rage and fear to come to the surface. The exercise below is a powerful way to allow your unconscious emotions to come forth in a safe way. If you practice this method regularly, your physical symptoms will begin to subside and, hopefully, disappear. When you give voice to the discomfort, it no longer has to hide in your body.

It's a brave act to allow subconscious
emotions like rage and fear
to come to the surface.

Rage on the page

One of the major spiritual pathways to freeing your body is through exposing impermissible feelings such as rage and fear. I started doing this practice after talking to my friend Nicole Sachs. Nicole is a therapist who specializes in the work of Dr. Sarno. When I mentioned I was struggling with TMJ, she told me about her journaling method that she recommends to everyone. She calls it "Journal Speak" and adapted it from Dr. Sarno. Nicole suggested that I journal for 20 minutes about all of my anger, rage, fear, and discomfort. Then, after 20 minutes of writing, she instructed me to meditate for 20 minutes to allow the emotional release to set in.

Ready to relieve my jaw tension, I was willing to do whatever she suggested.

I made a few of my own tweaks to the practice as she described it. For one, I renamed it Rage on the Page. Then I decided to add bilateral music. Bilateral music rhythmically stimulates each side of the brain to help fully process thoughts. It opens our "window of tolerance," which is the psychological state when we're best able to respond to whatever comes our way by building emotional resilience. Emotional resilience increases our ability to process stress and big emotions, keeping them from getting stuck in our subconscious.

Twenty minutes of Rage on the Page brings your unconscious rage and fear (or worry, sadness, judgment, or any other repressed emotions) to the surface. Then, in your meditation, while listening to the bilateral music (found at DearGabby.com/HappyResources), you allow yourself to become more present with those feelings so you can take the tension and pressure off your body.

Note: You may resist the idea of putting your rage on the page because you were taught as a child that it's wrong or unsafe to feel angry or afraid. Many people grew up with parents who repeatedly said, "You're fine; let's move on" or shushed you when you cried. Even these simple remarks can create the belief that it isn't safe to feel discomfort. Many parents haven't worked through their own emotional distress and, therefore, cannot hold space to experience a child's emotions. When a child's emotions are repressed, they can form a belief that it is not safe to express anger, rage, sadness, or other forms of distress. This results in an ego perception that we must do anything we can to avoid those impermissible feelings.

When we release our unconscious emotional distress, we clear our energy field and return to emotional balance.

Nevertheless, you may find that this process is too much for you at this time. My friend Sarah did this practice and it was too activating. After the 20-minute practice of raging on the page, she felt scared that she let herself "go there," as she put it. Sarah was brought up in a home where no one ever talked about their feelings. She'd never seen either of her parents cry (even when close friends or family members passed away). Sarah's emotions, too, had been repressed for decades. So when she started to rage on the page, she was terrified and ashamed by what was coming through. Shame is a common response to expressing how we truly feel if our emotions were repressed as children.

Once I was able to help Sarah calm down, we both agreed that Rage on the Page wasn't right for her at that time. I suggested that she come back to it when she'd done more of the work I share in this book and felt safer to face big emotions. If Sarah's story sounds familiar, feel free to skip this practice right now and return to it when you feel ready. Alternatively, test-drive this practice with less charged emotions such as a minor annoyance or frustration. Sometimes the small stuff reveals the big stuff. So starting off lighter can be very effective. Do what feels safe, and don't push yourself. If for any reason your intuition is telling you that this may bring up too much for you, then save it for another time. Throughout the book, I will continue to share self-regulating practices to help you support your nervous system. You can always return to these practices when you feel stable enough to process them.

As challenging as Rage on the Page may seem, it may make it easier if you remember that no one will see this journal—this practice is an opportunity to give voice to repressed emotions. Also keep in mind that journal entries about anger will not manifest more negativity into your life. It is quite the opposite. When we release our unconscious emotional distress, we clear our energy field and return to emotional balance. In this state we become a Super Attractor, spiritually aligned and a magnet for what we desire.

The Rage on the Page Practice

1. **Turn off your phone so you'll be uninterrupted, then set a timer for 20 minutes.** Press play on the bilateral music (links at DearGabby.com/HappyResources). Flip your phone over so you aren't watching the timer.

2. **Open your journal and write for 20 minutes** (you may need to start with 5 minutes and build up). Journal about anything that's been triggering you—from your anger about an ex-boyfriend to frustration about a disappointing breakfast. There's no issue too big, too small, or in any way off-limits. Let it all out onto the page: rage, anger, frustration, fear, worry,

doubt. Remember, if you feel resistance to this process, take it slowly and start by journaling minor annoyances rather than major emotional distress.

3. **When the timer ends, stop writing.** Adjust your position to make sure you're sitting comfortably.

4. **Gently close your eyes and continue listening to the bilateral music.** Let whatever feelings need to come up move through you.

5. **Just breathe, and feel your feelings.** Follow this breath pattern: Breathe in deeply through your nose as your diaphragm extends. Exhale completely out of your mouth as it relaxes.

6. **When thoughts come into your mind, gently let them pass through and let them go.** This meditation is a free-flowing practice of breathing deeply and exhaling completely. Let the music take you on a restorative journey.

    Meditate for as long as you wish. It doesn't have to be 20 minutes at first. Do what you can, and every time you return to this practice, meditate for a bit longer until you're at 20 minutes.

If, for any reason, this practice triggers you or makes you uncomfortable, you can visit DearGabby.com/HappyResources for more therapeutic support. Take care of yourself, and do what feels good. If this practice supports you, the best way to get great relief is to make it a daily habit. After practicing Rage on the Page for over a year, I now turn to my journal in any moment of distress and release any unconscious emotion so it doesn't get repressed and stuck in my body.

The body comes out of hiding

Now that I have this practice as part of my daily routine, I'm able to release unconscious negative emotions before they become physical conditions. My life is different as a result. I feel serene in a new way. I live with perfect digestion, free from anxiety, and my physical tension has subsided. I sleep nine hours a night because I'm no longer suppressing emotions. My jaw is relaxing (big one for me!), and I'm moving through difficult experiences with grace.

The concept that your physical conditions could be psychosomatic might still feel hard for you to believe. Don't overthink it. The next time you feel your back pain flare up, your stomach go into knots, or that same old migraine take hold, ask yourself what you need to feel. Then give yourself the necessary time to practice journaling whatever rage, fear, anxiety, or other emotions need to come through. Don't judge what comes up; just let it out. Then, following your journaling practice, meditate and allow your body to relax. I'm confident you'll notice a shift in your body.

Find subconscious support

This writing practice can also support you through experiences of emotional upheaval like the death of a loved one, a breakup, or some other tragic event. Often we want to run from those deep feelings, but giving voice to them is what sets us free. I have even used this practice to help me deal with managing my team at work. For over a decade, I worked very closely with a woman I considered to be like family. But as my career got bigger, our relationship dynamic changed. I began to sense her resistance to me on calls and in meetings. Eventually I called it out with love, but that didn't seem to resolve the issue. Sometime later she resigned with a short and curt e-mail.

My initial reaction was outrage. I went right into protector mode, started trying to find her replacement, and blamed her for the pain I was feeling. Then I pulled myself together and spoke with her over the phone. I was able to tell her how much our friendship and work relationship meant to me and how painful it was for it to end in this way. She responded, "It's just time for me to move on, Gabby. That's it." Her unemotional response left me sad, frustrated, and without resolution. So I took my rage to the page.

After 15 minutes of journaling about how angry and outraged I was, the truth came out. I began to sob as I wrote about how this current experience reflected my deep childhood wound of attachment breach and abandonment. I journaled on and on about the pain of being abandoned and my deep-rooted belief that I was always at fault. I was able to come out of my meditation with a new perspective. The moment I was able to honor my childhood triggers I could recognize hers. I could recognize her suffering and honor her experiences and decisions. But most important, I could come one step closer to honoring my child self, who had felt neglected. (We will go further into this in upcoming chapters.) Practicing Rage on the Page helped me release the unconscious anger rather than store it in my body.

Affirm how you want to feel

One of the most powerful ways to ease your emotional distress (and therefore your physical symptoms) in the moment is to use positive affirmations. Louise Hay taught the power of positive affirmations as a spiritual tool for reorganizing your thoughts and beliefs and also your energy field. When you affirm a positive desired feeling, you begin to lean into what is possible and you become present in the moment. Louise said, "The point of power is always in the present moment." Positive affirmations can ground you in the present by giving you an elevated point of focus. When repeated, they can become a mantra that can dissolve all fearful thoughts with love. Words alone have the power to change your energy field and therefore your body. Creating a practice of reciting positive affirmations is a transformational way to bring your thoughts, energy, and body back to peace. When you notice a thought, a physical symptom, or a trigger arise, turn to any of the following positive affirmations to guide you back to grace. If you want to enjoy my positive affirmation meditation, you can visit DearGabby.com/HappyResources.

I am safe in my body.

Everything is working out for me; I am truly taken care of.

I am at ease.

I am free in my mind and body.

The Universe has my back.

I can let go and trust that everything is unfolding perfectly.

My presence is my power.

My energy is powerful.

My body is strong and resilient.

I am still. I am well.

You can even make up your own positive affirmations that resonate with you. One affirmation that always supported me at some of my darkest times is "Everything is happening around me; I am truly taken care of." Affirming this always made me feel at peace and reminded me of the spiritual presence within and around me. Years later I return to that affirmation whenever I notice tension in my body.

Don't underestimate the power of positive affirmations. Return to this practice whenever you notice tension or fear rise up. This is a fast and spiritual way to release your subconscious and return to the truth of who you are. Choose an affirmation that makes you feel at peace and recite it daily.

The promise

Spiritual and psychological truths have the power to offer great relief and freedom. The goal is for you to recognize how powerful your stress response is and to notice when you're triggered into a state of emotional distress. The more aware you become of your physical sensations, the more you are able to shine light on your subconscious emotions. While you may not yet be able to face all the feelings that dwell under the surface, your willingness to acknowledge their presence is yet another step forward. Let your body be your guide to revealing what truly needs to be healed.

Let your body be your guide to revealing what truly needs to be healed.

It's also possible that just by acknowledging your unresolved emotions, your body has tensed up. That's okay, and it's common. For now, just notice the form of your physical response. Give yourself permission to go slowly, and know that you do not have to resolve all of your emotions overnight. If for a moment each day you can let your physical symptoms be a reminder to turn inward, breathe, journal, and feel, then you're on the right track.

As I write this chapter, I'm in awe of how my affirmation became my reality. Everything is truly happening around me and I am truly taken care of. My calm state has allowed my body to heal. My chronic physical issues have been naturally resolved through addressing the underlying emotional triggers. Giving my emotions a voice has set my body free.

Be open to miracles, and trust that your body is revealing to you what you need to heal. In no way do I want to dismiss chronic illness or pain, although I cannot overemphasize the benefits of lowering your stress response. When you become willing and safe enough to allow your subconscious emotions to come to the surface for healing, then your life will change forever. Your stress responses will subside, your nervous system will relax, and your body will naturally heal itself.

Trust that the practices in the coming chapters will continue to unlock the hidden emotions that have been running the show. Setting them free to be healed and resolved will be the catalyst for emotional and physical relief. Take this one step at a time, and follow my lead.

CHAPTER 5

Speaking the Unspeakable

Still early on in my trauma recovery, I connected with my speaking coach, Gail. We got on the phone to chat about one of my upcoming talks. I opened up to her about the trauma.

"Gail, I feel that I have a responsibility to speak out about this," I told her. "One in three women are sexually abused, and I want to help people release their trauma."

"I understand your desire to serve, but you are not ready," she replied. "If you share this too soon, you will trigger your audiences and maybe even retraumatize yourself."

I understood her concern and promised that I wouldn't share about it too soon.

Soon thereafter, I started to prepare for an upcoming talk. And for the first time in my career as a speaker, I was terrified to get onstage. While I'd made a promise to Gail that I wouldn't give a talk on my unresolved trauma, I don't always know what is going to come out of my mouth. Once I got onto the stage, I was in my "home zone," as Gail calls it. I felt spiritual inspiration speaking through me, which always provided me with a rush of oxytocin. I felt present, I felt safe, and I felt in control.

I joyfully made it through the talk and then headed into the Q&A. The third person to ask a question was a young woman who bravely shared about childhood sexual abuse. For years, I'd witnessed people vulnerably sharing like this. But today it felt different. Today, her vulnerability was mine. Her terror was mine. Her trauma was mine. She asked for guidance on how to move forward while being stuck in a state of post-traumatic stress disorder (PTSD). Without thinking, I leaned into the microphone and said, "One in three—including me. You're not alone, my friend. Remember that you are not alone." I could see relief come over her as soon as she realized that I, too, was a trauma survivor. In that instance I felt good that I had the opportunity to help this young woman know she wasn't alone in her suffering.

The moment I got off the stage, however, negative feelings flooded over me. I barely made it through the book signing. As soon as I was done, I got into a cab and went home to crawl under the covers and cry. Gail was right, of course. I shared too soon. I couldn't pinpoint the feeling I was having. I didn't understand it. I was so overwhelmed, paralyzed, and afraid. Publicly admitting my trauma seriously activated me.

Publicly admitting my trauma seriously activated me. I was so overwhelmed, paralyzed, and afraid.

A humble moment

Now, nine months after remembering the trauma, I'd built my therapeutic team and I was on a mission to heal. This was when I started to direct my awareness toward the "Warrior" part of my personality. The Warrior, as I called her, was the hard-charging part of me, ready for a challenge. It was the fearless part of me that got on a stage with a microphone three months into my sober recovery. The bold part of me that vulnerably shared my truth to audiences of strangers. The driven part of me that was devoted to helping others transform and heal.

Around this time, a friend of mine invited me to cohost a weekend workshop for women. Feeling stronger because of the months of therapeutic work, I was eager to get back onstage and serve others. So I said yes to sharing the stage with two other teachers and I looked forward to being in a room filled with women. I thought I was signing up to teach, but little did I know that the Universe was guiding me to learn.

In the morning session, I sat back as one of the other teachers led the group. She began to speak about shame. As I sat and listened, I started to feel triggered. Most of the room looked like I was feeling. When the presenter suggested that we were feeling uncomfortable because we were avoiding shame, I got defensive. I thought of myself as a confident person who had overcome so much. What did I have to be ashamed of? Then she suggested we team up with a partner to practice an exercise about shame. And for the first time in my life, I came face-to-face with the core reason I was running. That impermissible, uncomfortable feeling I'd worked so hard to avoid. The most terrifying emotion of all: shame.

> For the first time in my life, I came face-to-face with the core reason I was running. That impermissible, uncomfortable feeling I'd worked so hard to avoid.

At first I felt relief, as though I'd found the missing piece to a puzzle I'd been trying to solve. Now that the puzzle was complete, major realizations began to set in about my triggers and reactions. I thought about how my immediate response to any issue was outward defense but inward blame. If my husband got mad at me for not helping around the house, I'd fight back and then within minutes blame myself for not being good enough. Or if something went wrong at work, I'd initially want to blame someone else, but then quickly return to my negative mantra, "I'm a piece of shit." Shame was underneath it all.

As I sat in that audience filled with other students, I realized how much I still had to learn. So much of my suffering came from all the ways I ran from the deepest feeling, the core wound of shame. I realized I had believed that it was easier to judge myself, judge others, overwork, drink, and even fall deep into spiritual practice, than it was to face the impermissible shame of what had happened to me.

The following week I brought this realization to my therapist. She looked on with compassion as I opened up about my recognition of shame. With an empathetic tone, she explained to me why the shame was there in the first place. She helped me see that shame was my response to the unexplained cutoff of attachment from a parent. My mother's erratic energy, my father's inability to connect to me, and the traumatic experiences that no one acknowledged or attended to. The day my mother abruptly left my father and told me that I had to help him tell my brother the news, I was only nine years old. All the ways in which my parents were unable to create a safe bond but instead established the perpetual feeling of neglect turned into chronic disappointment from which I could never rebound. As a child I felt left alone to manage my feelings. My parents would often say, "There she goes again; Gabby's having another tantrum." Each time one of my parents would cut off their connection to me in an abrupt way like that, I'd go further down the path of believing my big feelings were my fault and that something was wrong with me. I believed that all the moments of parental disconnection and cutoff were my fault. I believed wholeheartedly that I was a piece of shit.

The origins of shame

In psychology, attachment theory posits that in the first two years of life it is imperative that a child have a strong bond to at least one primary caregiver. It is critical to our development. When bonding is strong and we are securely attached, we feel confident to explore the world, knowing that there is someone we can safely return to. If the bond is insecurely attached, we are afraid to leave or explore, unsure of our ability to return. Securely attached people tend to trust others, and on balance have an easier time navigating life. The insecure attachment is a form of trauma that can affect the direction of a child's life if it remains unresolved. (More on attachment in Chapter 9.)

Even one abrupt cutoff, such as a parent laughing off a child's meltdown or bursting out in rage when the child spills milk, can trigger shame in the moment. That shame can be resolved with a quick repair, honoring the child's feelings and apologizing for the mistake. But when cutoffs are repeatedly left unrepaired, it can turn into chronic shame.

Even writing these words right now triggers my shame. I feel ashamed that my emotions weren't acknowledged. I feel ashamed that I didn't have a safe place to turn to when I was in distress. I feel shame carrying the memories of abuse. I can face that shame today, but for over three decades, I ran from it.

In efforts to avoid the feeling of shame, I built up a story about my childhood that was far different from reality. My story consisted of an amicable divorce. I'd always say that I had hippie parents who were able to maintain a healthy friendship, and that I grew up comfortable enough in a wealthy town. Never would I admit that my family struggled financially, or that at times my mother's small apartment had a renter occupying one of the bedrooms. I believed in the story that my childhood was happy and that I was safe. I had to create this story in order to survive the shameful truth about my childhood.

Hardwired for connection

No human is immune to the ubiquitous emotion of shame. As it turns out, shame is a neurobiological response to feeling abandoned, which Edward Tronick, Ph.D., director of the Child Development Unit at the University of Massachusetts Boston and an associate professor at the Harvard University School of Public Health, revealed in a powerful study performed in 1975 called the Still Face Experiment.[1] The premise behind the experiment was to demonstrate that babies are extremely responsive to the reactivity, emotions, and social interaction that they receive from those around them.

The experiment was set up with seven pairs of mothers and children. Each mother sat across from her child playing, laughing, cooing, and smiling. The baby pointed, laughed, and played along. They were deeply engaged and having fun. Then the mother turns her head away and looks back at the baby with a still face. For two minutes she stares at the baby with no expression on her face. At first, the baby tries to get the mother's attention by smiling, pointing, and laughing. Then the baby starts to become distressed, and she throws up her hands in the air and looks away. Soon thereafter the baby begins to cry and shriek—anything to get the mother's attention. The little baby then loses control of her posture while the crying continues. Finally, after two minutes, the mother smiles again and reestablishes connection. The baby immediately shows signs of relief and smiles along. This profound experiment helped demonstrate how babies are hardwired to establish connection, and when that connection is lost, the emergence of distress, shame, and fear becomes visible.

Shame is one way children establish an emotional bridge with their parents. Shame can keep us safe by reinforcing the biological need to seek a caregiver when we are young (and otherwise helpless). The neurobiological purpose of shame is to keep us out of danger and protected by our parents. So when we notice a parent disconnect, the shame response has us do anything we can to get that connection back.

So while shame is a natural response, when it becomes chronic and unresolved it results in trauma to the nervous system. It happens both from childhood events and from our experiences as adults. When a boss, partner, or family member constantly activates a stress response in us (through words, actions, or behaviors that scare us), the normal shame response can move from healthy to traumatic just as it would have during attachment breach in childhood.

Avoiding shame at all costs

We have many ways of building up safety mechanisms to avoid our shame. One example involves my friend Billy. He grew up in what looked like a healthy home. Although Billy didn't know it, his mother suffered from a great deal of unresolved trauma. She didn't have the ability to handle negativity or uncomfortable feelings—neither hers nor Billy's. The moment unsettling issues came up, she would try to move as quickly as she could to reestablish positivity without acknowledging any of the problems. So Billy never felt that his emotions were seen or heard. This (inadvertent) dismissal of his big emotions unconsciously sent Billy into a place of shame and disconnection from his mother. In his adult life, Billy sought out intense emotional connections in romantic relationships to fill the need to have his feelings validated. Each relationship would seem as extreme as a drug addiction. And when a relationship would end, Billy was left feeling unsafe and alone, which led to deep depression.

In his late 30s, Billy came to me for help. I took an inventory of his past and his relationships with his parents. As I began to touch on the topic of shame, like all of us, he desperately didn't want to consider it. Billy had lived for decades not even contemplating that he carried any shame. This is because shame hits the core wounds of feeling unlovable and inadequate. Fortunately, Billy was willing to do anything to find some relief from his addictive emotional relationships, so we kept talking.

"Give me an example of when you feel you need to defend your emotions."

He knew the answer right away! He told me that he became infuriated when people casually called him crazy. Like when a friend would say, "You're so crazy in relationships."

"How does it make you feel?"

"It makes me feel misunderstood, like I'm too much." Crying, he added, "It really makes me feel ashamed of my emotions and not emotionally taken care of." And there it was, Billy's shame. As we talked more, Billy realized that he was severely ashamed of having feelings his mother had spent decades trying to shut down. He had anesthetized that shame by finding romantic partners who shared his same need to have big emotions. Those relationships gave him a type of freedom and permission to act out all of his feelings. But the more emotional the relationship was, and the more he was drawn to it, the more dysfunctional it became.

You may relate to Billy's story and find relief in knowing that many of us act out in a way that avoids the shame we felt as a child. Or you may feel resistant to the concept that shame could be driving your life choices. That's okay.

Take a deep breath and be present with any feelings that are coming up. I'm here with you every step of the way. Each word in this book is infused with my love and compassion for your journey. As I write this, I am intentionally sending healing energy into the manuscript. I'm holding you in a safe container to dip in and dip out of these uncomfortable emotions. You don't have to experience it all at once.

If you can discover where shame may be hiding, then you have the opportunity to face it and move past it, rather than unconsciously letting it rule your life.

If you can discover where shame may be hiding, then you have the opportunity to face it and move past it, rather than unconsciously letting it rule your life. Sometimes the fastest way to identify shame is to look closely at our reactions to it. Outlined below are the five common reactions to feeling ashamed as taught by my Somatic Experiencing practitioner Brian Mahan. (I'll go into more detail about Somatic Experiencing in Chapter 8.) You may identify yourself in one or more of these reactions.

1. **Attack the other**

   One way people (including me) respond to feeling shame is by attacking the person who activated the feeling. It's common to project out what we don't want to feel. It's like playing a game of hot potato, quickly turning around to blame and criticize right back. I lived most of my life in this cycle: When criticized or triggered into a feeling of shame, I'd attack back in an effort to deflect the feeling away . . .

2. **Attack yourself**

   Another reaction to shame is the inner critic. It's a core belief that "there's something wrong with me." That underlying belief system creates thoughts like: *I deserved it. They were right. I'm bad. I'm toxic.* And in my case, I would go as far as *I'm a piece of shit.* I would initially attack back and then quickly move into self-attack and self-blame.

3. **Deny**

   Denial is a form of dissociation, a way of checking out. In this case, the shame is too much to handle, too painful. Dissociation is a survival mechanism to help one gain distance and space from unbearable feelings. When someone dissociates from shame, they will often create new storylines for the underlying event. For instance, when I first remembered the trauma, I'd justify or rationalize my story by saying things like, "It didn't happen. My childhood wasn't so bad." I even found myself saying out loud to friends, "So many people have had it so much worse than me."

Denial is also an addict's coping mechanism. Addiction is a form of denying deep-rooted shame. As addicts, we use drugs, sex, love, alcohol, work, gambling, and other addictive patterns to anesthetize the discomfort of shame. Other forms of denial include going into a state of numbness or blankness. I experienced this at times in therapy when we'd turn to a topic that was too shameful for me to face. I would literally begin to fall asleep. This was my brain's way of shutting down the shame response.

4. **Fawn and cling**

Another way of dissociating from shame is to cling to another person and establish a connection. Fawning and clinging to the person and continually saying, "I'll be better," is a childlike shame response that is reenacted as an adult. Unresolved shame triggers child parts of ourselves that feel like they have to make things right for the parent figure.

5. **Withdraw**

   This occurs when someone pulls inward, licking their wounds in isolation. The withdrawn person cannot trust anyone, loses faith and hope. This response can lead to depression and suicidal thoughts. It can also result in the desire to attack, in an effort to fight against the suffering.

The body reacts to shame

Shame is an instinctual response rooted in a physiological experience. Brian Mahan says, "Shame is an embodied belief that 'something is wrong with me.' Because shame exists in the body as well as in the mind, it must be treated somatically." In my therapeutic experience of addressing shame, it became clear that I couldn't just heal it psychologically. I had to allow my body to reveal the shame to me by looking at the physical symptoms that weren't resolved. My unresolved shame kept me stuck in a state of hypervigilance that kept my nervous system from regulating naturally. I was always on high alert, ready to protect and attack, protecting myself from having to experience the shame. This heightened state of arousal felt like perpetual panic always in the background no matter what was going on.

Stephen Porges, author of *The Polyvagal Theory*, teaches that shame, like trauma, is a parasympathetic shutdown and freeze. This is what happens physiologically:

1. The moment we experience shame in the presence of another person, we will automatically cut off social engagement by breaking eye contact. Our head can tilt as

we dissociate and disconnect. Our posture may hunch, shoulders roll forward, and our chest concaves. Our pelvis can tuck in as we disengage.

2. Our brain gets scrambled, and the larynx constricts to stop us from saying what we were going to say.

3. Then the body freezes, bracing and collapsing in self-protection.

These physiological responses may sound familiar to you. Feeling shamed is a threatening, fearful experience. Without realizing it, every time we experience shame, it sends the message "I am not safe" to the nervous system. That threat ignites a sympathetic charge that can be more than our nervous system can tolerate. At this point, the parasympathetic nervous system tries to contain the charge. This can present like a freeze response. But underneath that freeze resides a tremendous amount of emotional energy in the form of fear, vulnerability, defensiveness, and sadness.

We all have unique physical responses to shame that come forward to protect us from the feeling of being unsafe. Some common bodily responses include feelings of disconnection from the body, numbness, dissociation from the current experience, and tightening of the jaw, chest, or throat.

Go easy

Our bodies work hard to protect us from the fright of shame. If you were to come out of the freeze state too fast, it would be like ripping off the lid of a pressure cooker. So be sure to go easy. If you feel triggered, take a deep breath and know that there is a gentle way out. However, if looking at your relationship to shame feels like too much, return to this chapter later. Bravely looking at the ways you've been avoiding shame can be uncomfortable and shouldn't be forced.

Accept that subtle shifts in your awareness can offer you a new and healthy relationship to your shame. If you feel up for it, follow my guidance to take a closer look at how shame may be running your life. I will guide you through spiritual practices that will help you counter shame and take away its power.

To help you move forward with the upcoming exercises, set the intention to honor your shame by seeing it through the lens of love. Let's start with a prayer to let love lead your healing path. (Remember, you can replace the word *Universe* with God, Spirit, Source, Love, Energy.)

Thank you, Universe, for helping me feel safe as I explore new emotions. Thank you for helping me grow and heal through the lens of love and dissolve self-judgment.

Use this prayer to anchor you back into the energy of love as you explore the methods outlined below.

Practice awareness

Shame is a pervasive feeling that we cannot avoid, but it can be reprocessed and transformed through techniques that interrupt the pattern. The first step to healing shame is to witness it. In your journal, identify which of the five shame responses—attacking others, attacking yourself, denying, fawning, or withdrawing—you most commonly use. Then, throughout the next few days, lovingly and compassionately notice when something triggers you into one of those responses. Since you've already identified your triggers and their underlying emotions, this exercise is about looking more closely at which of those emotions are disguising shame, such as fear of rejection, feeling unsafe, or feeling unworthy, unlovable, or inadequate. Some common beliefs tied to shame can be *I'm useless, I'm a failure, I don't deserve anything good*, and on and on. Your willingness to recognize the patterns and be inquisitive about shame is an act of self-respect. You cannot heal what you're unwilling to see.

You cannot heal what you're unwilling to see.

Even though I couldn't recognize or admit the shame at first, I would commonly say, "No one can take care of me. I have to fix it all myself." Recognizing my two most common shame responses helped me see how the feeling of being out of control triggered childhood memories of being neglected and expected to take care of myself. Unpacking this pattern further, I noticed that when I felt out of control I also felt helpless and unsafe—but ashamed that I couldn't do anything about it.

Accepting yourself

Accepting that we all face shame is the first step to accepting it for yourself. Firstly, remind yourself that shame is a normal physiological experience. You didn't create your shame; it's part of the human condition. So acknowledge that you are not alone in your shame. We all suffer from it, and we all have the power to transform it.

You didn't create your shame; it's part of
the human condition. We all suffer from it,
and we all have the power to transform it.

Secondly, it can be helpful to remember that "healthy" shame is a biological way of protecting a relational connection. As children, shame kept us ever looking for a strong connection with our caregiver. As adults, healthy shame helps us see when we've hurt others or broken an interpersonal bridge. Establishing a healthy relationship to our shame supports our connection to others by helping us see our part and apologizing when necessary. Finally, a healthy relationship to shame allows us to explore deeper vulnerable emotions that can be brought to the surface for healing. The goal isn't to get rid of shame, but to use it as a barometer for our relational connections and unhealed wounds.

Your willingness to open up to the concept of shame means that you're on the precipice of a radical transformation. Your willingness to witness and transform this painful emotion moves you toward freedom and brings real relief.

Becoming grounded and steady

Now that you've done the profound work of acknowledging your shame response and, therefore, your shame, it's time to discover some tools that will help you reassess and reframe childhood shame that you've carried for decades. These methods will help you face the shame from a resourced, grounded, steady state. Resourcing is anything that gives you a sense of well-being, safety, or pleasantness. For some people, when they notice a shame reaction, it can be helpful to envision that they are on a beach, in a beautiful forest, or with a close friend who makes them feel safe. Ground yourself by leaning into anything that can give you a sense of well-being in the moment.

When I first began to think about my shame, I noticed how quickly I would dissociate from the feelings and how my body would go numb. At times, I even felt like I was floating out of my body. So I found these practices a helpful way to stay connected to my body. If you're feeling out of control or afraid, allow these practices below to help you ground yourself in a safe place.

1. **A power pose.**

    Stand up and get your body into Wonder Woman or Superman pose. Get into a strong stance with your legs shoulder width apart and put your hands on your hips. Roll your shoulders back, and lift your chin up slightly. Settle into the feelings that arise as you stand in this posture. This pose is great for raising inner strength and confidence. A *Psychological Science* study in 2010 showed that assuming a power pose before a meeting can boost your self-confidence and even change your hormone levels.[2]

    I practice the power pose whenever I prepare to get onto the stage and present. Getting into this stance frees up my energy and instantly makes me feel a sense of inner strength and confidence.

2. **Grounding your body.**

    Rub the palms of your hands together or tap your feet gently on the floor.
    Breathe deeply.

On the exhale, push your hands down on your thighs.

On the inhale, pull up on your thighs.

Repeat five times.

Tap your feet gently on the floor or rub your hands together again.

This simple method will help you feel grounded in your body.

These tools will help you get back to a resourced state in the midst of a shame reaction. Once you are grounded, then you can move into facing shame through a loving lens.

My Somatic Experience teacher, Brian Mahan, coined the term *flawsome*—flawed and awesome. "When one is flawsome, they have the ability to recognize and acknowledge that we all have flaws and that we can still be good people," he says. So let's start by accepting that with all of your history, stories, and shameful feelings, you are flawsome! Then take a moment to be proud of yourself for having the bravery to look at your shame and the willingness to move forward. It may feel scary, but it's such a loving act of self-care. When we bring our shadows to the light, then they can be healed.

When we bring our shadows to the light, then they can be healed.

Self-compassion

Once I was able to identify and accept that I had shame, I began to speak compassionately to my shame. Right now, lovingly remind yourself that you are not your shame. Even if you don't yet know the root cause, become willing to see yourself in a new light. Here are some affirmations to repeat to self-soothe in moments of shame:

- I am not my shame.
- I am safe and loved.
- I honor my feelings and allow myself to feel them now.
- I'm doing a great job caring for my feelings.
- My big feelings are beautiful.

I understand that even saying those words to yourself may be triggering. Self-compassion can be difficult for people who have pervasive shame. Even tiny bits of self-compassion can feel forbidden. If you're struggling to find compassion for yourself, try finding compassion toward someone else who's had a similar experience. By seeing love in them you will be reminded of the love within you.

Experiencing compassion can melt away the shame. Compassion is the antidote to shame. When we align our energy with the love of the Universe through prayer, meditation, affirmations, and self-compassion, we open up our consciousness to see ourselves in the light of who we truly are. Even after taking a moment to practice compassion for yourself, you may still feel entrenched in shame or self-loathing. Let yourself off the hook for how you feel. Say to yourself in that moment, "Shame is a natural emotion." Self-compassion can melt away shame.

Self-compassion can melt away shame.

Shame is terrifying to face, so if you feel overwhelmed, numb, or even agitated, that's okay. Don't judge or deny any of your feelings at this moment. Continue to take these concepts and practices at your own pace, and never push past your own comfort level. Establishing a healthy relationship with your shame must be done slowly and with the right support. My hope is that you are now open to the possibility that you no longer need to stay stuck in the shame-freeze or a constant state of self-protection. I'm proud of you. I hope you can feel it through the page. You've started healing the deepest wound that will lead to the greatest freedom and peace. Giving voice to your shame is the first step to releasing its grip.

Giving voice to your shame is the first step to releasing its grip.

CHAPTER 6

Don't Call Me Crazy

It's May 12, 2019, Mother's Day. I'm sitting in the back seat of our car next to my four-month-old son as my husband drives us to brunch at my in-laws' house. I look out the window, holding my breath with tears slowly rolling down my face. I whisper under my breath so my husband won't hear me, "I want to die."

I'm suffering and afraid to admit it. For more than a month, I've had daily panic attacks, nightly insomnia, agoraphobia, and severe depression. I've tried every tool in my spiritual toolbox, praying daily on my knees, therapy sessions, meditation, and every herbal sleep aid that is allowed while breastfeeding. I'm desperate for solutions to a problem that I'm not willing to admit is there.

When we arrive at my in-laws' house, I sit down at the kitchen table with my sister-in-law Meredith. I burst into tears. My mother-in-law comes over to the table and pats me on the back. "It's okay, honey, all new moms are anxious," she says. I know she's trying to help, and I love her for that, but this anxiety isn't just a "new mom" thing. For weeks, I have been white-knuckling it through the most difficult time in my life. Months of no sleep. Days filled with tears, breastfeeding, and sheer terror.

One week later, I head to Manhattan with my family because I have a talk the next day. That night I don't sleep, not even a minute. I move from the sofa to the bed to the loft and back to the sofa. I toss and turn, counting down the hours. The clock is my worst enemy. Around 6, the morning light shines through the window shades. I lie on my living room floor as tears fill my eyes. I am broken.

I roll over, pick up my phone, and send an e-mail to the event coordinator: "I'm so sorry to do this, but I'm really suffering with insomnia and anxiety. I'm not sure what's going on, but I haven't slept the entire night. I've never done this in over 15 years as a speaker, but I need to cancel my talk." I press send. Then the shame and guilt set in. I don't feel relief; I feel like a piece of shit.

Then I text my therapist. This is a daily routine. "Sorry to bother you again so early in the morning. I don't know what to do anymore. I haven't slept in weeks, and I canceled my talk this morning. Call me when you can."

The clock turns 7:30, and my son begins to cry. I go into the bedroom to change his diaper and sit him down to feed. My husband looks at me with sad eyes. He's traumatized by all I've been through and terrified that there is no solution. As I feed my son, I sob and say to my husband, "I canceled the talk. I'm a piece of shit, and I may as well die."

As I finish nursing Oliver, my phone rings. It's my therapist. "We need to talk," she says. "Please get Zach on the phone." I put the phone on speaker, and we huddle around to hear what she has to say. "Gabby, your tools are no longer working. I believe you are suffering from postpartum depression and anxiety. I am suggesting that you speak to a psychiatrist and get on medication. This is a biochemical condition that you cannot fix on your own." I'd spent months dreading this diagnosis, but for some reason the moment she said it out loud, I felt relief. I took a breath of acceptance. Sometimes intervention is the only way for us to truly accept what's really going on.

When I saw a postpartum psychiatrist, she diagnosed me on the spot and put me on a medicated path. Medication was new for me. I was brought up homeopathic. I had never had a prescription filled in my life. But when I walked out of the doctor's office with the prescription in my hand, I felt immediate relief. I got in a cab and headed right to the pharmacy to pick up my medication. Zach met me. We stood there holding hands with hope in our eyes. When we went to dinner that night, I was the happiest I'd been in months. I hadn't yet taken even one pill, but just knowing they were there was enough to make me smile.

Later that week I checked in with my friends, acupuncturists, and healers who had been helping me. I admitted to them how severe my condition was and shared my diagnosis: "I'm going on an antidepressant. Don't worry, it's a super low dose. Hopefully, I can get off of it soon." I found myself justifying it because I felt so ashamed that I couldn't fix this with my spiritual practices or holistic lifestyle. Then I shamed myself for not being over the shame.

I found myself justifying medication because I felt so ashamed that I couldn't fix my postpartum depression with my spiritual practices or holistic lifestyle.

The most important thing my psychiatrist said was: "Gabby, you've done a lot of trauma healing, spiritual practices, and therapeutic work. Now with medication, you will feel safer, which will allow you to go even deeper with your therapy. This will be a blessing for you." I held on to her words. I made the commitment to use the medication as a tool to help me fearlessly go deeper into the therapeutic work. I wasn't going to just take a pill and numb out. I was going to go deep and use my new baseline of safety to transform the memories that I'd been so frightened to face.

Accepting my diagnosis

The following week, I had to lead a workshop for hundreds of people at a spiritual center in Massachusetts. Two of my best friends, Robyn and Jamie, came along. I told them that I needed a babysitter—for myself. I was one week into my psychopharmacology path, but not yet sleeping. (It often takes months to get the right therapeutic dose of the medication.) I needed support from friends I could trust and rely on in case I had insomnia or a panic attack.

The first night of the retreat I excused myself around 9 P.M. to bathe and try to wind down for bed. I clung tightly to a stuffed monkey that I'd taken from my son's nursery that had become my security at night. As the minutes rolled by, I felt the surge of anxiety spike in my chest. Finally, I grabbed Monkey and ran across the hall to Robyn and Jamie's room.

"Robyn, you take my room, and I'll sleep in here with Jamie. I need to feel safe." Robyn happily moved across to my room. I spent 30 minutes tossing and turning in Jamie's room before I grabbed Monkey and walked back to my room to get into bed with Robyn. Then I grabbed Monkey one more time and headed back to Jamie's room again. I looked at my friends with terror in my eyes and said, "Please don't call me crazy." Robyn smiled and said, "You're not crazy. But Monkey didn't sign up for this!" We all laughed in the midst of the chaos.

I only slept one hour that night. I couldn't put on a happy face and pretend I was okay the next day. The only way to get through the full-day workshop was to tell the truth. I got on the stage that morning, and my eyes welled up with tears. I told an audience of strangers that I was suffering from post-partum anxiety and depression, that I was newly diagnosed and on medication. I talked about my insomnia and how I hadn't slept the night before. I even cracked a joke about Monkey. The audience extended love and positive energy my way. I felt held and comforted by these compassionate souls. Telling the truth required a lot of self-compassion. What I experienced that day was a reminder that compassion is the antidote to shame.

Telling the truth required a lot of self-compassion. Compassion is the antidote to shame.

A few months later, I was at the right dose of the antidepressant. The panic had subsided, the insomnia was under control, and I was out of the depression. With my new baseline of safety, I was ready to continue facing the truth of the abuse, the shame of neglect, the impermissible rage, and the terror that lived in my body. I became a student of transformational trauma healing therapies. My doctor was right. The medication gave me a new baseline of safety that would allow me to go even deeper with the therapeutic work. I went far with EMDR therapy, which gave me the ability to recover new memories while safely resolving them. Through the practice of EFT, I was able to regulate my nervous system on my own, which helped me establish a new level of resilience. I will describe both of these therapeutic modalities in great detail shortly.

I came to understand that the abuse and neglect from my childhood had shrunk my window of tolerance (my nervous system's ability to ebb and flow in and out of big emotions without getting emotionally flooded). *Window of tolerance* is a term coined by Dr. Daniel Siegel (more on Siegel's work later in the book). With an optimal window of tolerance, we're able to regulate our nervous system naturally. Even in moments when we're extremely upset or distraught, our nervous system can get activated and then naturally settle. When a person has experienced chronic trauma or insecure attachment, the window of tolerance shrinks and the individual has less ability to ebb and flow out of emotional states, becoming overwhelmed and triggered more easily. The medication and deeper therapy, particularly EMDR, helped expand my window of tolerance. For the first time in my life, I was starting to feel safe. In that place of safety, my constant state of sympathetic arousal was transformed to a parasympathetic state in which my nervous system relaxed.

The stigmas that hold us back

Even though I'd begun to feel relief on the medication, I still held on to the shame about it. I felt ashamed to share my postpartum experience with other moms because deep down I felt like a failure. Everyone says having a baby is the best time of your life. For me, it was the scariest. I felt ashamed when I spoke about the medication with my spiritual friends because I hadn't been able to heal myself through spiritual practices or natural remedies. Some of my contemporaries and fellow authors have stood on stages and written books denouncing antidepressants. This made me think that medication was off limits, especially for a spiritual teacher.

What I was most ashamed of, though, was that for over a decade as a teacher, I too was unwittingly contributing to the stigma. I'd stood on stages and responded to questions about mental illness in ways that no longer resonated. In a kind and compassionate way, I'd say things like, "Here's a breath practice for anxiety" or "Meditate more and your depression will lift." While I believe wholeheartedly that meditation is a solution, what I didn't realize was that these comments were potentially unhelpful to anyone suffering with severe mental health issues. I didn't understand how trauma affects the brain, or what it was like to have a biochemical condition that required medicated support.

Years before my own diagnosis, I'd asked two women on my team to write a blog for my website about their anxiety journeys. One of the women included a paragraph about how antidepressants saved her life. After reading it, I felt concerned that it would bring up a debate about medication on the blog, so I asked her to remove it, making the case for keeping a potential controversy out of the blog. At that time I felt justified, but little did I know that I was shaming a team member I cared for and contributing to the stigma.

Thankfully, years later I was able to make amends. On the exact day that I picked up my own medication from the pharmacy, I called her to apologize. I told her about what had been going on with me and the relief I felt to be on a medicated path. Luckily, I found a supportive voice on the other side of that call.

A loaded topic

This is not a PSA for antidepressants, but it's also not a topic to ignore. We live in a culture (especially in America) where drugs are highly overprescribed. I understand the side effects inherent in antidepressants and other psychopharmaceutical medications. But many people who've experienced unresolved trauma, depression, postpartum depression, severe anxiety, bipolar disorder, or any other form of anxiety/depression know what a miracle medication can be. In certain cases, it saves lives. Medication when prescribed as part of a larger program of recovery and therapy really can help you get to a safe baseline where you can start to do the deeper work.

Medication can help you get to a safe baseline where you can be calm enough to do the deeper work.

Take your mental health seriously, and consciously make decisions based on educated psychiatric guidance. With a proper diagnosis from a qualified physician, trust that you are being guided on a healing path. Do your research, and don't rush to get medicated without thoughtful communication with your psychiatrist. (If you're a mother struggling with postpartum depression or someone concerned about a possible mental illness, visit DearGabby.com/HappyResources for guidance.)

I share my medication story to take away the stigma. If you had a heart condition, you wouldn't flinch before taking prescribed blood thinners. When you're suffering from an acute mental illness, it's important to seek psychiatric guidance and get support. But it's a starting point, not the destination. Keep going; the deeper healing happens in therapy, spiritual practice, and your own commitment to reprogramming your emotional and physiological state. Therapeutic healing is what's required for true freedom, and it's the key to regulating, reprogramming your brain, and retraining your nervous system.

From a spiritual perspective, God is in all healing devices, whether it be medication, a doctor, or a therapist. When we are in the pursuit of freedom and are willing to do whatever it takes to get better, we will always be guided to the exact healing methods we need. Seeing the medication in this way, recognizing it as part of God's plan, helped me release the shame and embrace every part of my healing journey.

The only way to fully recover from addiction is to address and heal the root cause of suffering from the past.

When I understood what happened to my brain in childhood, as an addict, and post-pregnancy, I had far more acceptance of myself, my experiences, and my inability to be present. I could see clearly how my brain's inability to take in information, focus, and keep me feeling safe was not my fault. I could see how the programming from my childhood had affected my neural pathways and, therefore, my life. When I began to understand how deprived of serotonin my brain had been because of chronic hypervigilance, I accepted the help of antidepressants for serotonin support. I no longer thought of myself as "crazy." Instead, I could lovingly accept my underdeveloped brain function and welcome the fact that I was spiritually guided in all ways, including the medicated path.

Rewiring the brain

Thankfully, the brain's neural pathways and synaptic connections have the ability to change and reorganize. This is known as neuroplasticity.[1] Through therapeutic methods and mindfulness practices, I could rewire my brain. I started noticing that my brain was changing when I was two years postpartum. By that point, I had fully recovered from the postpartum depression and anxiety. I had spent over a year supported by medication, which helped me establish a new baseline of safety and restored my brain's reserves. Most important, I'd dived into therapeutic practices for rewiring my brain.

My amygdala's alarm response no longer reacted to situations that previously would have triggered me. Instead, I was able to witness my frustration or discomfort, be compassionate toward myself, and lovingly guide myself back to peace. In addition, I felt safer in my body, which made me feel more secure in every area of my life. My brain functioned differently, so much so that I became interested in using my mind in ways I'd never imagined. For instance, the research it took to write this book wouldn't have been possible previously. The fact that I looked forward to reading trauma books and attending training courses were testaments to my brain's new capacity to take in information. Witnessing my resilience and my ability to heal helped me speak up about the stigmas that had kept me from getting the support I needed. My hope is that a deeper understanding of your past, what it does to your brain, and how it affects your behavior will help you see yourself and your circumstances (no matter how dire they may be) with compassion and love.

My spiritual practice became stronger too. The more at ease I became in my day-to-day life, the more I could access a direct connection to the spiritual realm. I could hear the internal dialogue of Spirit more clearly because I was no longer moving so fast in such a heightened state of fear. In stillness we receive the Universal guidance of love as a clear direction. The more grounded I became, the more connected I felt. Spirit was always with me throughout my life but now I felt the presence of love become more integrated. This deeper spiritual connection allowed me to show up at my highest capacity as a teacher, wife, friend, and mother.

In stillness we receive the Universal guidance of love as a clear direction.

A safe way to reprocess your past

With Spirit by my side, I felt safe to go even further on my healing path with the support of Eye Movement Desensitization and Reprocessing. This transformational therapy uses bilateral stimulation for trauma, which engages the subconscious brain in healing and processing strong emotions. When practicing EMDR you don't have to figure out why you're having a reaction, physical symptom, or behavioral pattern. Instead, through the support of a therapist and bilateral stimulation (accomplished with certain hand movement, audible headphone buzzers, or left-to-right eye movement), you can access and process traumatic memories and other adverse experiences and bring them to an adaptive resolution. Typically, a therapist starts an EMDR session by asking you to think of an image related to a specific memory, as well as any associated negative beliefs, emotions, and body sensations.

When applying EMDR to a minor disturbance or type of phobia (a nontraumatic event), one can often feel relief within eight sessions. When working with trauma, additional sessions are usually required, but some relief can happen much more quickly. That was the case for me. I felt immediate relief with EMDR, and I continue to practice it to this day. EMDR helped me to safely unlock the fragmented memories and set my unconscious mind free from the trauma.

The first experience I had with EMDR was just five months into my trauma therapy. I was scheduled to fly to Los Angeles for a very important work event. There was no way that I wanted to miss it, but at that moment I couldn't contemplate how I'd even get in the car to the airport. I called my therapist for help. "Meet me at my office at 7 A.M. tomorrow. We will do an EMDR session and it will help you get on the plane." We had been talking about EMDR therapy for a few weeks.

Early that next morning, my therapist handed me buzzers to hold in each hand and began asking me a series of questions. She was helping me identify the target for the session. She explained that the target didn't need to be about the trauma, it could simply be about whatever I was struggling with that day. My target was clear: I was afraid to get on the plane. I turned on the buzzers and surrendered to her guidance. She followed my responses and asked leading questions that would help me connect to my feelings. As the time went on, my body began to shake as if I was discharging energy from my body. She told me that this was normal and not to be alarmed. I went with it and allowed my body to move in whatever way was necessary to clear the stagnant energy. Before I knew it, the session was complete. I turned off the buzzers and opened my eyes. The room was brighter, and I felt relieved.

"Do you feel safe to get on the airplane tonight?" she asked.

"Yes, I'm ready."

I walked out of her office and fearlessly got into the elevator (I'd been afraid to take the elevator for months). Then I walked out onto Fifth Avenue with a sense of safety greater than I'd felt since remembering the trauma. I got on the plane that night.

The relief I experienced from this profound psychiatric healing approach made me want more of it. What I love most about EMDR is how spiritual it is. As the Universe would have it, I was guided to an EMDR specialist who helped me go even further in the process. Her ability to intuitively guide me to explore unresolved memories and emotions was a spiritual process. It was as if she was attuning with my energy to allow Spirit to work through her to guide me. I have always believed that Spirit works through people (particularly therapists, doctors, and healers). And in this case, I felt truly guided by a force of love working effortlessly through this woman. Often I would see sparks of light flash behind her chair. This was a common experience for me in therapy sessions. Those sparks of light are angels and Spirit guides peeking through to let me know that I'm in the presence of a healer. Whenever I'd see a spark light up, I'd know Spirit was working through my therapist to help me heal.

EMDR is one of the most powerful tools for feeling relief fast. If you feel called to look more into EMDR, take your time choosing a therapist to work with. Make sure you feel safe with them and that you sense their ability to connect to you energetically, not just through your words. To work with an EMDR practitioner, visit DearGabby.com/HappyResources.

Self-regulation techniques you can do on your own

If you cannot receive EMDR support (or even if you can), I highly recommend exploring Emotional Freedom Techniques, also known as Tapping. EFT is a psychological acupressure technique that supports emotional health. It's a valuable self-regulating technique for PTSD, anxiety, or other forms of mental instability. And it's something you can do at home by yourself. Much like EMDR, EFT is a spiritual and psychological practice. At times it can even feel meditative, and it works on the subconscious level to allow you to feel great relief without emotional discomfort. It doesn't require effort, only willingness. When you practice EFT on your own or with a practitioner, you can always trust that there is spiritual guidance by your side.

How EFT works

The goal of EFT is to balance disturbances in your energy field. More than 5,000 years ago, the Chinese identified a series of energy circuits that run through the body, which they called meridians. This concept forms the basis for acupuncture and acupressure healing modalities.

EFT combines the cognitive benefits of therapy with the physical benefits of acupuncture to restore your energy and heal your emotions. Unlike acupuncture, EFT doesn't use needles. Instead, you stimulate certain meridian points on the upper body (seen in the diagram on the next page) by tapping on them with your fingertips.

When you tap on specific energy meridians found on your face, head, arm, and chest, you can change neural pathways and clear out the emotional disturbances behind addictive habits, phobias, triggered reactivity, and more.

Tapping can help release old fears, limiting beliefs, negative patterns, and even physical pain. While you tap, you talk out loud about the issue you are working to heal. Allowing yourself to emote while simultaneously tapping on the energy points sends a signal to the brain that it's safe to relax. Our fear response (controlled by the amygdala) then lowers. I've found that tapping on anxiety can be one of the most profound ways to regulate my nervous system and get back to a safe baseline.

TAPPING POINTS

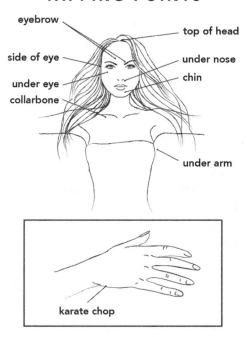

Figure 1. EFT Meridians

You start with what's called the most pressing issue, or MPI. Next, rate your pre-tapping MPI on a scale of 0 to 10, 10 being the most distressing. This number gives you a point to refer back to after your session and help determine its effectiveness. Then you start tapping, beginning with "negative rounds" and moving on to "positive rounds." You talk as you tap on the different meridian points.

You'll see how EFT works and get the hang of it quickly with the EFT script on anxiety below. If you want to follow along with me on video, go to the resources page at DearGabby.com/HappyResources, where I've also included a video on tapping for shame and another for tapping on anxiety. This process will give you relief and lower your anxiety. But it's important to note that tapping can sometimes activate you. If at any point you feel overwhelmed by the tapping, continue to tap but let go of the script and instead repeat these words: "I am safe. I am safe" while you tap. If the idea of facing your shame or even giving voice to it feels too overwhelming, please skip this practice for now.

Tapping for shame

For this tapping exercise, let's start by using the following pressing issue: "I feel ashamed of my past." My hope is that this practice will help you feel safer in your body and more accepting of your story. (And while this might not be your most pressing issue, it will give you a chance to learn the practice. At that point, you can go back and amend the statement.)

Round 1:

Rate your MPI before we start on a scale of 0 to 10 (10 being the most severe).

Now review the diagram for the tapping points.

Side of the hand (KC: karate chop): Even though I feel so ashamed of my past, I deeply and completely love and accept myself. (Say this three times.)

Eyebrow (EB): I'm so ashamed of my past.

Side of eye (SE): I don't want to accept myself.

Under eye (UE): I don't want to look at the past.

Under nose (UN): What will I do? How will I handle that?

Chin (CP): It's all up to me, and I'm feeling overwhelmed.

Collarbone (CB): I wish I could calm down.

Under arm (UA): I'm so ashamed of my past.

Top of head (TH): I want to push this away because I can't stand the thought of facing it.

Take a deep breath and rate your MPI.

Round 2:

KC: Even though I'm so ashamed of my past, I deeply and completely love and accept myself. (Say this three times.)

EB: It's scary to face this shame.

SE: But I've gotten through scary things before.

UE: I know speaking my truth offers me freedom.

UN: Maybe I just need to take a break and vent.

CP: Maybe I can get relief from this tapping session that I'm doing now.

CB: I do know I'm not alone in my suffering.

UA: I know I can calm down eventually, and I welcome that shift.

TH: I honor my experience and accept myself and my situation completely.

Take a deep breath and rate your MPI.

Round 3:

KC: Even though I'm ashamed of my past, I choose to be calm, confident, and relaxed. (Say this three times.)

EB: Calm, confident, and relaxed.

SE: I choose to know that I am not alone.

UE: I choose to be accepting of myself, my past, and my present.

UN: I choose to be calm, confident, and relaxed.

CP: Calming down now, relaxing my body.

CB: It feels good to take a break and feel calm.

UA: I am compassionate toward myself.

TH: I accept myself and my situation completely and I love myself. I'm safe.

Take a deep breath and rate your MPI.

Notice how you feel and honor the shifts that occurred.

When you're done tapping, rate your MPI (most pressing issue) on a scale of 0 to 10. Has it decreased? Typically, when you practice EFT, your MPI can be lowered significantly in just one session. When it comes to deeper topics like shame, there is the possibility that you'll stay at a high number or even go up. If that happened to you, please practice any one of the grounding tools from Chapter 5 to calm your energy.

**Tapping is intended to bring you relief
and help you process unresolved emotions.**

Speak your truth

A powerful way to shift the shame from the past is to speak your truth in the present. Giving your experiences a voice can be extremely liberating. One of the reasons why Alcoholics Anonymous is so successful in helping people with addiction is because it's a safe place to speak your truth—and, importantly, to recognize your truth in another human. The more we speak up about our suffering, the more we contribute to ending the stigma and shifting the shame. We can no longer suffer in silence.

Giving voice to your mental illness, depression, addiction, anxiety, trauma, abuse, or anything that caused you harm can feel terrifying. I understand, but I want you to consider that it's far more terrifying to live in hiding or suffer in silence. The metaphysical text *A Course in Miracles* says, "And yet it is only the hidden that can terrify, not for what it is, but for its hiddenness."[2]

Hiding your truth is like living in your own self-inflicted prison. Speaking truth sets you free.

To be clear, I'm not recommending you speak up about something before it's too soon. But I am suggesting that you write about it for yourself. The practice of accepting yourself fully through the written word can be a first step to speaking your truth. Take a moment (maybe after tapping) to write freely about your experience. Admit your truth on the page. This could be the first time you even admit it to yourself. Remember, it took me months to admit that I was suffering from a biochemical condition and get the help I needed. Had I read a chapter like this and given myself permission to accept my suffering, I might have gotten help much faster. Fearlessly acknowledging your suffering is a form of prayer. Consciously or unconsciously, you're asking for a miracle. You're inviting the presence of Spirit to take the wheel and show you what to do.

You must admit your truth to yourself before you can speak about it. Give yourself full permission to write freely about what you feel, what you need, and what you've been through. Don't be afraid to use words like *addiction*, *abuse*, *mental illness*. Take away the stigma for yourself.

A powerful way to shift the shame from the past is to speak your truth in the present.

You are not alone

The healthier I've become, the more comfortable I am talking about trauma and addiction recovery, my medicated path, and my postpartum experience. The more I heal, the less shame I have around these topics. I believe that my willingness to speak about these topics has allowed other people to release their own shame. When you hear someone tell your story, you no longer feel alone. When you witness someone bravely give voice to their truth, your shame can dissolve. You can recognize yourself in the other and no longer feel so alone. I've felt that connection to people all throughout my healing journey. In 12-step rooms I'd be surrounded by people whose lives were drastically different from mine, but inside we were the same. Seeing your sameness in my story or in the stories of others will greatly benefit your healing path.

My commitment to shifting the shame around these topics led me to dedicate an episode of my podcast, *Dear Gabby*, to stopping the stigma and shifting the shame around mental health and trauma (you can listen to the episode at the resources link DearGabby.com/HappyResources). My intention for that episode was to help you recognize that you're not alone in any of the experiences that have left you with shameful feelings or emotional distress. Suffering is a universal experience, but we often think we're alone in it. Knowing you're not alone in your experiences can help you stop suffering in silence so you can honor your truth. I want you to give voice to the unspoken shame that the world has told you not to face. The first step to shifting shame is to give voice to it, to speak on behalf of it, to honor and hold people in their experience of mental illness. If we don't speak on behalf of it, then we will stay silent. We will stay stuck. We will stay frozen in time.

My new baseline

It's been three years since my postpartum diagnosis, and I've never felt more at peace. In retrospect, I can honor that terrifying experience of my childhood as a catalyst for my greatest growth. I was able to establish a new baseline of safety through understanding my neurobiology and accepting psychiatric support. I finally felt safe enough to take my recovery to the next level to reprocess the memories and triggers that had kept me stuck in reactive patterns. I could undo my reactivity and face my triggers with more grace and resources. Most of all, I was able to dismantle the wall of shame and fear that had held me back from peace.

If you're struggling right now with chronic pain, addiction, anxiety, or mental illness of any kind, please know that by following this guidance you, too, can look back one day and see it as a great gift. When we face our discomfort with faith instead of fear, we can grow in profound ways. It's faith that got me out of the darkness, and it's faith that keeps me in the light.

It's faith that got me out of the darkness,
and it's faith that keeps me in the light.

CHAPTER 7

Love Every Part

I'm back on my therapist's sofa staring at the ceiling. As I listen to the sound of the window-unit air conditioner, the honking of horns on Fifth Avenue, and the noise machine in the hallway, I stare at her diplomas on the wall and the bookshelf. I wonder if she's read all of those books. I wonder which books are her favorite. My mind wanders so I don't have to face the fact that I'm there to face myself. Ugh, I dread these sessions.

Even now, after all the work I've done, there are still more layers of the onion to peel back. Work to do. Whenever my therapist tries to go deeper, my body freezes, my shoulders slouch, and I feel nothing. The moment she asks me about my feelings, I can no longer feel anything. I dissociate. When I check out, she checks in more. She asks me a series of questions that make me want to crawl out of my skin. She suggests that there is a "protector" part of me that's masking deeper feelings. She asks if the "protector" can step aside and whether I know anything about the part of me that I am protecting: "What part of you needs to feel safe in this moment?"

I don't know who the eff the protector is protecting. And I definitely don't know what that "part" of me needs to feel safe. No one has ever asked me that question. Safety isn't a feeling I've contemplated. So I go numb. Often, I stay there for most of the session.

For some reason, this day was different. She gently kept at it, continuing to ask me how young the part of me was that I was now trying to protect. I kept resisting. She remained patient but wouldn't let me change the subject. Her persistence made me uncomfortable enough to get out of my numbness. I felt something. I was pissed off. Noticing my feelings, I released some resistance. Upon witnessing my energetic shift, she asked me to check in with how I was feeling in my body. I allowed myself to feel frustration and discomfort. I noticed how my body reacted to that feeling: My shoulders slouched, my jaw tightened, the lower half of my body went numb, I crossed my arms, and my head tilted to the side. Witnessing myself in this position revealed the hidden part—the little girl I'd been protecting. "I'm ten, and I'm scared. I feel shame. I feel anger. I don't want to talk about it." I started to speak in a childlike tone. The protector part of me had stepped aside to give voice to the little girl.

The dialogue with my 10-year-old self didn't last long before I checked out again. The moment my therapist acknowledged the little girl, she didn't want to be seen. So there I was again, numb, yawning, and avoiding the shame. My therapist asked me why it felt so unbearable to acknowledge the little girl. I told her that I never wanted anyone to see her. It didn't feel safe. My therapist explained that I had never felt safe enough to let the protector step aside. The miracle that day was that for even a moment I was able to give voice to the scared and ashamed 10-year-old girl. I was able to touch into the child part of myself that had been hiding for so long. This was the beginning of a newfound awareness that would change my perception of myself forever.

A new self-perception

I didn't realize it at the time, but my therapist was practicing Internal Family Systems (IFS) therapy created by Richard Schwartz, Ph.D.* This is an approach to psychotherapy that works under the premise that we have multiple "parts" of who we are that show up at different times. Here's a simplified explanation: Perhaps you notice a critical part of yourself show up when you make a mistake at work, or an outraged, aggressive part of yourself freak out whenever you're frustrated with your spouse. It's likely that throughout your life you've even referred to these different parts without realizing it, saying something like, "Whenever someone tells me I'm wrong, there's a part of me that becomes outraged and fights back." While you may have referred to these behaviors as different parts, it's unlikely that you ever perceived them as distinct personalities. It's more likely that you thought of these parts as emotions or as justified reactions to outside events. In IFS therapy, the concept is that our big reactions and emotions are actually parts of us that show up to protect us from feeling deeper wounded parts (often younger unresolved parts).

In a conversation with a friend about IFS, I started to explain that we have all of these different parts of ourselves. "No we don't, we are one complex personality," she said. That's a common response. This concept may seem like a lot to take in at first. It isn't what we've been taught to believe about ourselves, so it can seem wrong to our logical mind. I can imagine that the idea of having different parts of yourself can be challenging, so I'm going to do my best to demystify it for you because IFS has been one of the

---

* Richard Schwartz, Ph.D., was a 32-year-old systemic family therapist at the time when he discovered IFS. In his treatment he noticed that his clients were describing various different parts within themselves. He also noticed that when clients felt safe with him and energetically regulated, they could access an undamaged core Self.

most transformational elements of my personal growth and trauma recovery.

Let's start by taking a look back at the trigger exercise from Chapter 2 and review the patterns in what triggers you and how you respond. Here was the example I shared in that chapter:

Trigger	Feeling	How I run from the feeling
Being out of control	I feel terrified. My stomach gets tight. My jaw clenches. Anxiety takes over.	I try to control other people and my surroundings. I overwork to the point of exhaustion in order to get back into a place of feeling in control.
When someone tells me to shush	I feel silently outraged and act defensive.	I defensively push back on the other person, trying to figure out why they would shut me down.

Now, instead of seeing your feelings and the way you react to them as behaviors, what if you consider them to be individual parts of who you are? For instance, what if I saw the scared feeling as a young part of me that feels threatened? And what if I saw the way I run from that feeling as a protective part of me that withdraws to stay safe?

Take a moment to contemplate that the ways you run from and manage your triggers are likely attempting to protect you from experiencing deeper feelings that were developed at a very young age. Those deeper feelings in IFS are called "exiled parts." These wounded child parts can be so unresolved and therefore so deeply painful that we will do anything we can to protect ourselves from facing them. That's where your "protector parts" come to manage those unresolved feelings. Working tirelessly to keep you from having to face those deep wounds, the "protector parts" put up a strong defense.

We all have exiles (often scared inner children) and protectors (the ways we react when triggered in an effort to manage the exiled feelings). For example, an exiled part may be based on a childhood experience of feeling abandoned. When the fear of abandonment is triggered, the protector part will withdraw love to temporarily secure a sense of control and therefore safety.

The exiled parts are often thought of as the wounded child parts that at some point experienced some serious form of adversity. Unresolved instances of substantial adversity can result in fear, anxiety, helplessness, rage, or a sense of being alone, unlovable, and inadequate. Depending on your situation, the adverse moments from your past may be hidden from your consciousness, like mine were for me. Conversely, exiled parts can form at any age following a traumatic experience. You may not even be aware of these uncomfortable exiles, like in Chapter 5 when I shared that I didn't even know I had shame. That shameful part of me that was hiding was an exiled wounded child that had been well hidden from my conscience. It takes time and courage and therapy to identify these exiled parts.

**It takes time and courageous therapy
to recognize the split-off parts of ourselves
that represent the programming, experiences,
and conditioning from childhood to the present.**

Working with these wounded exiles is a very gentle process that requires the support of a trained IFS practitioner (found at DearGabby.com/HappyResources). So it won't be addressed directly in this book. For now, all I ask is that you acknowledge the idea that when you're triggered it's likely activating an unresolved, burdened, wounded part of yourself. At this moment, that part is safe and there is nothing we need to do with it.

The protector parts are the parts of us that show up to manage the exiles and keep them under control so we don't have to face the impermissible feelings of our exiled past. Extreme attachment injury with a primary caregiver or other childhood trauma can make us lose trust in others; therefore the protector parts do whatever they can to keep the exiled parts safe from those impermissible feelings. Protectors establish the unhealthy role of parenting and caring for the exiled parts. As they grow older, child exiled parts rely on the protectors to keep them safe. The unconscious mind is terrified by the exiled parts and fears that they could be triggered at any moment into anger, panic, shame, anxiety, depression, worthlessness, and even grief. Therefore, the protectors are always on standby, ready to keep the unconscious triggers from being revealed.

As seen in the recap from Chapter 2, protector parts are often associated with the ways we run or fight back. For instance, when someone puts you down, you get triggered into feelings of inadequacy. The way you respond to that put-down with rage and defensiveness is a protector part trying to save you from facing the deep-rooted feeling of shame or inadequacy. Your protector parts can present as rageful outbursts, controlling behavior, obsessive thoughts, judgment, and addictive patterns that can lead to drug, alcohol, and other kinds of abuse.

In a recent conversation with a young woman I mentor, she opened up to me about her binge eating. This wise young woman knew exactly why she binged. "I eat so I don't have to feel the shit from my childhood," she said, identifying that the part of her that binged was there to protect her from an exiled child self.

The protectors are always on high alert, warding off unwanted emotions. You may have always believed these were justified reactions, but from an IFS perspective they are parts of you that showed up for you at a young age. As you read this, you may be able to identify one or more of your protector parts. Maybe you're well aware of the outraged part of you that shows up around authority figures. Or the part of you that fights back any time you feel judged. Or, like the young woman I mentor, you may have a protector that uses addictive patterns like binging or drinking to put out the fire of big feelings, like grief or depression.

Even reading about the concept of exiles can trigger a protector. You may notice a protector part show up right now. Maybe you're yawning and feeling numb. Or maybe you're annoyed by this chapter and want to blame me for making you feel uncomfortable. It's totally understandable that your protectors would show up. They come swooping in the moment an exiled part feels triggered. It is all reflective of our inability to connect to our deeper emotions and instead we manage the feelings with defensive and reactive behavior.

Protectors are always on standby, ready to keep the unconscious triggers from being revealed.

My journey with IFS

My therapist and I worked together to explore my parts and even name them. For instance, I named one of my protectors "Knives Out." This protector showed up any time someone spoke to me with a judgmental tone. The moment I feel judged, Knives Out immediately goes on the defensive. Whereas "the Controller" shows up to protect me from feeling the frenzy of emotions that rise up when I feel out of control. Both of these parts have worked tirelessly to protect an exiled part I call "Little Gabby," the abused little girl who felt worthless and alone.

In the early days of the pandemic, my protectors were working overtime to keep the exiles at bay. I tried to control every detail of what was going on. In retrospect, I can also see that my activated protector parts were triggering protectors in my team. This was not a healthy dynamic.

Both Knives Out and the Controller proved to be trouble at work. I brought up the issue with my therapist and told her how I was acting at work. She said, "It sounds like your ten-year-old protector is showing up to try to help you feel safe when you're out of control. You probably don't want her to sneak in and try to run your business." Being able to laugh and honor my 10-year-old protector was a miracle. Instead of being shunned, she needed to be recognized.

Acknowledging my ten-year-old and her triggers was a major act of self-care and recovery. By fully acknowledging my protector parts I could more easily notice when they showed up. Then I was able to help them calm down and step back in the moment, thereby helping them be less extreme and activated.

Your undamaged Self

In therapy sessions when he was first exploring the idea of parts, Schwartz found that when his patients' parts felt safe and were allowed to relax, the patients would spontaneously experience confidence, openness, and compassion. This loving and compassionate adult part is what Schwartz then referred to as the Self (with a capital *S*). In IFS, the Self represents the undamaged, resourced, enlightened essence of who we are. Self is compassionate, wise, loving, and accepting of all of our parts, almost like a healthy parental figure. This Self knows how to take care of our exiles and protector parts. The qualities of Self are described by eight *C* words: *calmness, clarity, confidence, curiosity, compassion, connectedness, creativity,* and *courage.* The goal of IFS is to access and live from Self embodying the qualities of the eight C's.

Think of your undamaged resourced Self as who you are at your best—unstressed, at peace, confident, and compassionate. If you're a parent, the Self is reflective of the part of you that can compassionately care for and love your child when they're in moments of distress. For instance, I recently had a conversation with my friend about something that was pissing him off at work. I asked him a simple question, "If your son was dealing with this issue, what would you tell him?" Without hesitation, he said, "Don't worry, Son, Daddy's got this." This response was his resourced Self speaking up.

Your resourced adult Self is who you are at your best when you are unstressed, at peace, confident, and compassionate.

"Can you say the same thing to yourself right now? Can you tell the triggered part of you that you're going to take care of him?" I replied.

At that moment, the concept of Self set in for my friend. He agreed to speak to and care for himself the same way he would effortlessly show up for his son. He could see that he had a resourced Self that could show up to care for his triggered child parts and their protectors. Even if you're not a parent, think about how you'd care for a loved one or show up for a friend. When you become conscious of what it feels like to be in the energy of Self, you can rely on Self to be a supportive leader for the exiles and protectors, bringing all the parts into harmony. We all have a confident, compassionate Self at the core of who we are, but we may have lost touch with it due to the many painful parts that take our energy and focus. Without a connection to Self, a traumatized person can become overly burdened by their protectors' actions. IFS therapy aims to help you learn to rely on Self to restore mental balance. When the Self steps up to lead, the other parts are able to calm down. Establishing connection and access to your resourced Self is the most empowering way to move through conflicts and honor big emotions. It's the most powerful way to bring your child parts back to safety.

We all have a confident, compassionate Self at the core of who we are.

Establishing a faithful connection to Self did not come overnight for me. I continued to spend therapy sessions avoiding exiled "Little Gabby" and all the shame she carried.

My protector parts were terrified of what would happen if I acknowledged her even slightly. The protectors managed the shame and the possibility of remembering more about the trauma. I hid these fragmented parts of myself in an effort to stay "safe," although hiding these parts provided a false sense of safety. The protector parts were actually keeping me stuck in a perpetual cycle of feeling unsafe because I had to work really hard to hold down the big emotions of the exiles.

But through my therapy, instead of shunning the exiled parts, I had become more connected with my resourced Self to help relieve my protectors from their extreme roles. The goal was to allow my resourced Self to become a parent-like figure that I could rely on. It was a tough concept for me to conceptualize—almost the same way it was hard for me in my early sobriety to define what God or the Universe or Spirit meant. My entire life I'd worked hard to manage all the exiled parts, and I was unfamiliar with what it felt like to be in my resourced Self, even though it was there all along. I accepted that the more aware I became of my resourced Self, the easier it would be to support the other parts.

Awareness was the beginning of establishing a healthy internal system. Part of the process was spending time just witnessing my parts. Whenever I felt triggered, I would return to the practice from Chapter 2 and take a closer look at what part was acting out. Then I'd notice how a protector would sweep in to manage the deep-rooted feelings. Whenever I'd take a moment to pause and ask the protectors to step aside, I could give my resourced Self permission to support the protectors and exiles.

In Chapter 9, I will help you identify your resourced Self so that you can begin the process of reparenting your internal family. For now, my goal is to help you recognize your protectors and help you thank them for the great service they have offered. While they may be extreme and uncomfortable, they have kept you safe. Recognizing and honoring these protector parts is the first step to helping them step aside.

Thank your protectors

According to Richard Schwartz, "There are no bad parts." Each part has an important role to play, and when they get out of their extreme roles, they become beneficial to us. As we become more aware of and comfortable with our parts, we can begin reorganizing our internal family system by learning to rely on the leader part, the Self.

Maya Angelou said, "Do the best you can until you know better. Then when you know better, do better." Your protector parts, while they may have played an extreme role, have done their best at keeping you from reliving painful experiences. They've worked tirelessly to keep you from becoming extremely overwhelmed by unresolved childhood experiences. They've protected you from facing old wounds that you may not have been safe enough or ready to accept at the moment. While your protectors have created challenges in your life, it's important to note that they have had a valuable role. Therefore the goal isn't to shame your protector parts but to befriend them and help them get out of their extreme role. For instance, as I've become more conscious of my protector parts, I can see when they are in extreme roles versus when they're actually doing a great job. On a recent work Zoom call I noticed the Controller part of me swoop in when I felt that an outside vendor was taking advantage of my company. Typically this part would freak out, yell, and try to fix the issue immediately. This time was different. Instead of freaking out, I took a signal from the Controller part that I should speak up and with less emotion simply ask for what I need. In this instance my protector part did a beautiful job of taking charge without overreacting.

With greater awareness of our protectors, we can learn to use them in a non-extreme way. One way to do so is by bringing conscious awareness to these parts. In doing so, you open up to a greater sense of self-compassion. For instance, while I'm working in my therapy to release the Controller from playing such an extreme role, I'm still grateful for her. When she shows up, I know there is underlying fear lurking below the surface. But I can take a signal from the Controller that I should speak up and ask for what I need. I can also call on that part of me when I'm getting ready for a big project, since that part of me is so good at getting things done. Once the Controller is no longer so extreme, she can actually be an asset. Sometimes people think that if they change these parts of themselves, they will lose their edge. I have found that by having more awareness of my parts, they can be far more effective in my work and personal life.

By bringing conscious awareness to the different parts of yourself, you open up to a greater sense of self-compassion.

Understanding your protectors and their important role will help you forgive your addictive patterns. It was the best you could do at the time to survive. In my conversation with Russell Brand on his podcast, *Under the Skin*, he shared a story with me that supported this thesis. In a period of his addiction recovery, his therapist suggested that he thank the part of him that was addicted, explaining that it had kept him safe from feeling extreme fear. Our addictive behavior doesn't make us horrible people; instead, addictive protector parts can be seen as doing their best to keep us safe. Getting high on an intensely emotional relationship; numbing out with sex, drugs, food, or alcohol; or using work to avoid feelings are among some of the tactics for anesthetizing the exiled parts. Becoming abstinent from addictive patterns is only one step toward recovery. The true resolution begins with accepting that protectors were doing the best they could. Healing for these parts and their addictions comes through devotional therapeutic support, possibly 12-step recovery, and IFS therapy to gently address the exiles and the extreme protector roles. As a sober woman who's been treated with IFS, I highly recommend it to any addict. Gain access to an IFS therapist at DearGabby.com/HappyResources.

I recognize as a recovering addict that living in an addictive state was destructive to me and to others, but today I can forgive myself for the past by acknowledging the important role my addiction played in keeping me safe when I had no other resources to rely on. When addiction can be respected as a form of protection, we can forgive ourselves for the past—and that will clear space for healing in the present.

When addiction can be respected as a form of protection, we can forgive ourselves for the past—and that will clear space for healing in the present.

IFS and spirituality

I found that practicing IFS strengthened my spiritual connection. In my spiritual teachings I've taught that the love of God is always within us but that each fear-based belief we built up from childhood separated us from that love. According to the metaphysical text *A Course in Miracles*, a mere thought of fear separated us from the love of God and that was the moment "we forgot to laugh." This was the moment the *Course* calls "the descent from magnitude into littleness."[1] One fearful experience separated us from love (God) and that fear continues to grow. One fear-based thought builds upon the next, separating us further from the presence of love, building up the "ego" belief systems of fear, scarcity, attack, judgment, guilt, shame, and so on. The ego works tirelessly to "protect" its identity and the beliefs in fear, judgment, and separation by projecting the fear of the past onto the present and into the future. The ego uses fear as a false sense of safety. To me, the ego represents the fragmented IFS parts of us that become so convinced of their fear stories that they take on their own personalities and qualities.

We can release the ego and return to love when we become the nonjudgmental witness of our fear and are willing to forgive our past. Forgiveness dismantles the wall of fearful beliefs that block the light and love of who we really are. Through the experience of forgiveness, fear dissolves and love is restored. IFS directly reflects this spiritual faith. In IFS, this is known as a sacred witnessing and honoring of every part. When we realize that our extreme behaviors are survival strategies rooted in past trauma, we become compassionate toward ourselves. The sacred act of witnessing this truth is a radical form of compassion that allows light to shine into the dark corners of our psyche.

The more we lean toward God or Self, the more we soften the edges of fear, lay down our protector parts, and return to love.

From a spiritual perspective, our true nature is God or love. In IFS, our true nature is Self. To me these are one and the same. When we live a spiritual life, we make the commitment to witness our ego and bring it to God for transformation. The same goes for IFS. Each time we witness a protector part, we clear space for Self to step in and lead us back to our truth. A strength in faith in God offers freedom from fear the same way faith in Self relieves us of the burdens of our extreme protector parts. When we forgive our fear, we're forgiving our protector parts for merely trying to keep us safe. Forgiving our protector parts for their extreme behavior allows us to remember the love of who we are. When protectors are seen through the lens of forgiveness, they are no longer something we must fight off but instead a part of us that we can compassionately embrace. The more we lean toward God or Self, the more we soften the edges of fear, lay down our protector parts, and return to love.

IFS has led me to deepen my forgiveness practice. I was able to forgive my parts and thank them for their hard work. For years, I judged my protectors and couldn't even acknowledge my exiles. Today, with my newfound compassion and love for all of my parts, I can easily forgive myself in the moment, notice the part, and turn to my resourced Self for support. Working with parts is a daily spiritual practice that has changed my life forever.

Through prayer, we temporarily suspend our fears and allow our thoughts to be guided back to love. In the case of IFS, each time we acknowledge and honor our parts, it's like we are saying a prayer that welcomes the resourced Self to show up and take the lead. I came to understand that my parts in their extreme roles had separated from love. By consciously connecting to my protector parts I was praying for support from Self. As time went on, I learned to rely on the Self and always know where to turn for support and direction. The more I let Self lead, the more I felt love surrounding me when an exiled child part arose. This is a spiritual practice.

A prayer to connect to Self

Place your right hand on your heart and your left hand on your belly. Take a deep breath in and release. Read this prayer silently to yourself or say it out loud:

At this moment, I honor all of my parts and thank them for their service. With curiosity and compassion I witness every part of me through the lens of love. I welcome the presence of my resourced Self to take the lead and care for every part of me.

Breathe into the feelings that arise from this prayer. Hold your heart as you breathe in and gently breathe out. For a moment allow yourself to surrender any residual shame or blame toward your parts and instead open your heart to witness them through the lens of love.

The more I lean into my connection to the loving energy of Self, the safer I feel. That love is a universal energy within every human. As I develop greater empathy for myself, I can more easily empathize with the wounded parts of others. I can see people in reactive states and instead of judging them, I can honor their triggered parts. The same sacred witnessing that I offer to my protectors I can now offer to others.

As I develop greater empathy for my parts,
I can more easily empathize with
the wounded parts of others.

Getting to know your protectors

I'm excited to introduce you to an IFS practice that you can do on your own to begin to connect to and honor your protectors. These practices are not intended to resolve any issues or replace any form of therapy. Perhaps you may find that these practices inspire you to further your journey with an IFS professional. What's here is designed to give you a greater awareness of your protectors (but not in any way touch on the exiles). Schwartz recommends that when you're first starting IFS without a therapist's guidance, it's best not to try to interact with the exiles. When an exile is triggered, it can be overwhelming and cause more feelings of insecurity. So please don't do any work with exiles unless you're in a therapeutic setting. (To get in contact with a trained IFS therapist, visit DearGabby.com/HappyResources.)

Getting to know, honor, and respect your protector parts will give you a great sense of self-compassion and acceptance. Acknowledging your protectors is also how you can honor and respect your experiences from the past and the ways you've tried to numb out any suffering. As we embark on the next practice, please note that there may be a protector part of you that wants to resist the exercise for fear of unearthing impermissible emotions. I get it—you've spent a lot of time protecting yourself from feelings of shame, guilt, and frustration. Take a deep breath and know that our aim is just to get to know your protectors. They don't have to stop doing what they're doing. We just want to honor them and become aware of the ways they have kept you safe to this point.

Be sure to go slowly with the practice below to learn what your protectors have to say.

Noticing your parts

This exercise is a gentle way to get to know one or more of your parts. If you're struggling emotionally, consult with your therapist or mental health care provider before you do this practice. If you would like to follow this practice with audio guidance, visit DearGabby.com/HappyResources for my audio download.

Get out a journal or piece of paper and a writing utensil. Follow my guidance through this meditation to check in with your protectors.

- Gently close your eyes and notice any thoughts that may be present in this moment. You may become aware of many thoughts coming through.

- Take a moment to listen to your thoughts. As you do, notice which thought you feel you may want to focus on.

- Gently land on one of the thoughts that draws your focus. It doesn't matter which thought you land on. Land on the thought that feels like something you'd like to get to know better or something you'd like to change.

- Get curious. What does the thought reveal about you? Notice any words, images, additional thoughts, body sensations, or strong emotional responses that come to mind.

- Now open your eyes and write down whatever you're noticing. You may feel called to describe your feelings, draw a picture, or write specific words. Take your time. Don't edit what you're writing. Write whatever comes to mind.

- When you feel complete in your writing, take a moment to read it over. Continue to notice any new sensations, thoughts, or emotions. Just notice. What do you hear? What is your writing saying to you? What information do you get from what you put onto the page?

- As you look closely, what part of you have you identified? Maybe give it a name. Notice how you feel toward it. What reaction do you have about it? As you notice that reaction, close your eyes and listen to what that reaction wants to reveal to you. Notice how that reaction makes you feel emotionally, physically, and mentally.

- Now open your eyes and write down what you noticed. Once again, let it all out onto the page. Now you've identified a second part.

- Look at the two parts to see if there is any relationship between them. Notice what comes up. No part operates in isolation. This is the beginning of noticing the relationship between parts.

- Journal about what you noticed about each individual part and what you noticed about their relationship to one another.

Becoming aware of some of your parts is a useful practice in getting to know your internal landscape.

The many benefits of IFS

Many of us go through life judging ourselves day after day. Years ago one of my audience members got up and said to a crowd of strangers, "I hate myself so much, and I say it all day long. Just this morning, I tripped on the sidewalk and called myself a fat piece of shit." The audience shifted uncomfortably when she said this—not because it was so unbelievable, but because it was far too familiar. Many people thanked her for admitting publicly what they would be too ashamed to admit to themselves—that they too had thoughts like this. Her ability to voice this shameful thought temporarily allowed her to see this "inner critic" (protector part) with love and compassion.

Getting to know, love, and proactively care for your parts can be the most loving relationship of your life. I've found many benefits to understanding and working with my parts. I can easily see myself and all of my parts with true compassion and acceptance. This practice can also help you more easily relate to the people you love, and to others in your life. You'll be able to witness negative behavior as a protector managing a young unhealed shadow that has lived in fear. The more you become aware of your own parts, the easier it will be to see this in others too. But I strongly suggest you don't start taking an inventory of those around you! When you read a book like this, you'll be tempted to detect the issues in others and want to confront them. This is especially true in intimate romantic relationships. It can be very difficult to coach or therapize a loved one. Do your best to keep your eyes on your own side of the road. Just stick to your own practice, shine your light, and be a force of inspiration for them.

Getting to know, love, and proactively care for your parts can be the most loving relationship of your life.

As soon as I developed an easily accessible relationship with my resourced Self, I could invite Self into any situation to calm down the protectors and the exiles and honor the family system. For example, I was able to witness the benefits of IFS when I was once again stuck in the same controlling pattern with my coworkers. Although this time I was able to compassionately witness my protector and let Self take over. I was on a call with my team planning business development ideas for the upcoming year when I shared with them my frustration around how a project was being managed. I was met with some pushback. Statements like "That's past us now; let's move on." Right away, I noticed a protector part of me jumped in to protect the exile that never felt acknowledged or understood. In this case, the protector part started fighting back and attempting to pull rank. My insistence on dwelling on the issue resulted in a heated debate and a wasted hour.

Shortly after the call, I took a moment to notice the parts that had come to the meeting. I could clearly see how the protector part was running the conversation to protect the exiled child part from feeling dismissed. Then I asked my resourced Self for help. I asked her to help me repair the situation with my team, but first to repair the feelings with my internal family. I began to speak back to myself and befriend my protectors: "Gabby, it's totally understandable that their perceived dismissiveness would trigger you. Let's honor that. What would your child part want to say to them to make sure your feelings are acknowledged?" Then I let my inner child respond, "I want them to know that I just needed a minute to be seen and heard. I just wanted them to acknowledge me."

As soon as I said those words out loud to myself, I was able to send an e-mail to share how I felt and request that next time we take a minute to acknowledge my experience. This was a miraculous moment, not just because I was able to clearly communicate my desires but because I was able to allow Self to guide me to a place of safety and speak up for my needs. I let my resourced Self create harmony.

It may take time to connect to or even acknowledge your resourced Self, as your protectors may still be in their extreme roles. But you've hopefully begun to consider your parts, to love them all, to thank them for the very important role they've played. These steps alone represent a radical act of acceptance and compassion. Let that sink in and relish in the feelings of relief.

Bringing Little Gabby back to safety

The IFS work I practiced weekly with my therapist was finally setting in. I was becoming more comfortable recognizing and honoring "Little Gabby." My protectors had started to step aside and were no longer ready to pounce at any sign of threat. Without even realizing it, my parts were beginning to work together with my resourced Self taking the lead.

One night it all fell into place. I was struggling to fall asleep, having watched the news close to bedtime instead of following my typical sleep hygiene routine. I started to feel anxious and lay awake in bed for over an hour. I became flooded with memories of the months I spent dealing with insomnia during the postpartum depression. Those memories activated me even more. My heart started to palpitate and my jaw clenched.

To calm myself down, I closed my eyes and connected to my breath. Breathing in for two strokes through my nose, out one stroke through my mouth. Breathing in. Breathing out. Then I thought to myself, *Who would I want to envision comforting me right now? Who could I go to?* I thought of my husband, my friends, and my therapist, none of whom I thought could save me in that moment. Then out of nowhere a vision came to me. I was holding my son in my arms and putting him to sleep. I saw myself gently swaying him back and forth, whispering prayers in his ear. Then the baby in my arms was no longer my son—it was me! I was lovingly rocking the baby version of myself. Within minutes, I was sound asleep.

That one experience was a turning point in my personal recovery and growth. I can call on my resourced Self to show up at any moment to soothe the protectors who want to stay in control of my emotions and nurture the exiles who need to be seen. I now understand what it means to let the Self lead. The relationship to Self is the most important relationship of my life. The more I strengthen my connection to the Self, the more I live in harmony and love every part.

CHAPTER 8

Freeing
What's Frozen

"Race you to the house," Zach said. I really wasn't in the mood to race, but hungry from our walk and eager to get home, I agreed. So I started off to run. But for some reason I couldn't. As I tried to accelerate, my legs turned to lead. I was unable to move any faster than a brisk walking pace. I laughed it off as I stood there watching my husband run up the hill, but deep down I was concerned.

I shared this experience with my friend Elisa, who was trained in a body-based therapy known as Somatic Experiencing, or SE. (*Somatic* means "of or relating to the body.") I intuitively knew she could help me understand what was going on. When I shared the story of how I couldn't run, she nodded with acknowledgment as if it was totally normal. She helped me understand that my body was revealing an old trauma response of immobility. She explained that during the childhood traumatic experience I was likely unable to complete the physical movement that my body naturally wanted to do at the time, namely run the hell out of there. Instead I froze.

Freezing was my brain's way of protecting me from experiencing the enormity of the event and my inability to fight or flee. The freeze occurs when our brains secrete chemicals that numb any physical and psychological pain from a traumatic event. My inability to complete my body's natural response could lead either to dissociation or to psychosis, which could have threatened my sanity. So the biological response of dissociation, and freezing, helped me survive.

Discovering more body work

I felt great relief hearing Elisa's explanation of my experience and became inspired to take the next step on my healing path: to thaw my frozen state and free my body from the trauma. I would do that with the support of SE therapy.

Dr. Peter Levine founded SE as a body-oriented approach to healing trauma and other stress disorders. While Elisa was getting her doctorate in psychology, she would excitedly tell me all about her SE studies. Dr. Levine's work personally touched Elisa, and she spoke of him as if he were a rock star.

Initially, when Elisa talked about SE, my eyes would glaze over. At that time I was totally disconnected from my body and I hadn't yet remembered the trauma. The moment Elisa would speak about the body's sensations and the trauma that lived in the body, I would shut down. I was too dissociated to identify with it. Little did I know that she was introducing me to a therapy that would one day change my life.

Nearly six years later, SE has become a transformative part of my therapeutic journey. I had spent 30 years unable to connect with my body or many of the simple pleasures of life because I was living in and out of hyperarousal and dissociation. In his book *In an Unspoken Voice*, Dr. Levine writes, "Trapped between feeling too much (overwhelmed or flooded) or feeling too little (shut down and numb) and unable to trust their sensations, traumatized people can lose their way."[1] As we have discussed, these intense visceral reactions to trauma (fight, flight, or freeze) are biological functions intended to protect us from temporary danger. When the danger has passed, these biological responses are meant to fully process and discharge. But when the danger is chronic and/or unresolved, the balance in the nervous system is not restored. When the balance isn't restored, a traumatized individual can be left in a state of chronic overwhelm or numbness.

Dr. Levine believes that trauma can be thought of as energy that gets locked in your body due to a real or perceived threat.[2] The healthy biological response to threat is to go from activation (sweating, heart rate rises, etc.) to action (run, flee, fight) to safety (breathing, releasing energy) to balance. In certain cases, however, this trauma energy gets "stuck" in the body. This can happen due to an unresolved state of fight, flight, or freeze survival.

When fight and flight are not options, we freeze and immobilize, like "playing dead." This makes us less of a target. However, this reaction is time-sensitive; in other words, it needs to run its course, and the massive energy that was prepared for fight or flight often gets discharged through shakes and trembling. If the immobility phase doesn't complete, then that charge stays trapped, and, from the body's perspective, it is still under threat. The Somatic Experiencing method works to release this stored energy and turn off the threat alarm that causes severe dysregulation and dissociation.[3]

Symptoms of undischarged traumatic stress can range from panic, anxiety, hyperactivity, and emotional flooding to digestive issues, chronic pain, hostility, or sleep problems. In addition, one may experience depression, exhaustion, disconnection, dissociation, pain, low blood pressure, or poor digestion. Resolution of the perceived threat rebalances the nervous system and alleviates these physical trauma responses.

Our bodies hold imprinted memories from our past experiences or traumatic events. Unresolved trauma of any kind remains stored in the brain and when triggered can re-create the physical response as if the past trauma is being relived in the present moment. To fully resolve the traumatic imprints, one must release the memories that are stuck in the body by working with the physical sensations that occurred in relation to those traumatic events. Therefore, practices like yoga, chi gong, and others are used to help people get "unstuck." When the stress is processed properly, it moves through the body and discharges. For me, sustainable, long-lasting relief became available only when my nervous system was restored to equilibrium. I had to reprogram my body's primitive survival instincts to feel ease in my body.

Our bodies hold imprinted memories from our past experiences or traumatic events.

Focusing on the body rather than the story

SE therapy reconnects you to your physical sensations in an effort to help you "reoccupy" the body. SE is based on what is called bottom-up processing, which puts the focus on the body rather than revisiting specific traumatic memories. Instead of trying to change thoughts and beliefs, an SE practitioner will ask you to look at various physical sensations, reactions, and related emotions.

While anxiety no longer plagued me and I felt far less triggered, the unconscious freeze state kept me holding on in my limbs and shoulders. I was able to notice my body tense whenever I felt out of control. This was my body revealing what was still unresolved in my nervous system.

In my SE sessions the practitioner was solely focused on the body rather than the story. The sessions would begin by helping me tune in to my physical sensations and where I felt emotions in my body. As I began to describe the sensations, my head began to move left and right as though I was trying to say no. The physical pattern set in and repeated itself over and over.

"Slow down the movement," he said. As I moved my head back and forth in slow motion, he asked, "What do you notice now?" By focusing on the subtle movement of my head and slowing it down, my body was able to metabolize and release the stuck energy while avoiding retraumatization. I was finally able to experience the biological completion, which released me from the daily reenactment of the fight-flight-freeze pattern of PTSD.

While I highly recommend embarking on SE with a trained practitioner (found at DearGabby.com/HappyResources), for now, let me introduce you to some SE methods that you can apply on your own to calm, soothe, and self-regulate when you experience a trigger or stress. These are easy exercises that will help you regulate your nervous system and allow your body's natural biological process of moving through arousal to discharge. These exercises will also support your sleep and overall immunity and lower your stress levels.

The felt sense

The ability to connect to and describe feelings in the body is known as the *felt sense*. Drawing on work begun in the 1960s, Eugene Gendlin coined the term *felt sense* in his 1978 book *Focusing*. Gendlin's work aimed to uncover which variables accounted for successful therapy. What he found was that the most important variable was a client's ability to reference their sensation-based feelings—their felt sense. The felt sense is a physical feeling. It's the stomach fluttering with happiness when you're falling in love. Or the feeling of excitement and joy rushing through you when you reunite with a close friend.

When someone is stuck in fear, the idea of feeling inner sensations can be challenging. When someone is suffering from PTSD, they are either dissociated/disembodied or in a state of hyperarousal—or in cases like mine, vacillating between both. Therefore, many people walk through life disembodied (disconnected from physical sensations). When we go through painful or traumatic experiences, it can be hard to tune in to our bodies. If you're living in a state of hyperarousal or suffering from PTSD symptoms of any kind, it can be challenging to connect to inner sensations. When I became safe enough to address the trauma in my body through SE, I could begin to contemplate inner sensations. SE allowed me to let my body heal the story so I could become whole again.

In the book *The Body Keeps the Score*, world-renowned psychiatrist, author, and trauma researcher Dr. Bessel van der Kolk teaches that overwhelming experiences (aka trauma with a *big T* or *small t*) affect us in ways that talk therapy alone cannot address. His work explores how bodywork like yoga, EMDR, and SE support the physiological effects of traumatic disturbances. Dr. van der Kolk says, "If you have a comfortable connection with your inner sensations—if you can trust them to give you accurate information—you will feel in charge of your body, your feelings, and yourself."[4]

What I love most about SE is there is no pressure to revisit old memories or even speak about the trauma.

Dr. Levine refers to trauma as the inability to be present. A traumatized individual is often disconnected from their inner sensations, and it's body connection that allows you to be fully present. The following practices may be supportive for you and are designed to guide you toward awareness of your felt sense.

If you're feeling safe and grounded enough to explore your inner landscape, then apply this gentle practice. It is not intended to look at any sensations related to trauma, just to provide awareness of your felt sense. If you find a traumatized part of the body during the exercise, simply redirect your focus onto a neutral or positive sensation. Or speak compassionately to yourself with words like "I'm here for you. I love you. I'm with you. I am supporting you." Go slowly; don't force yourself into any inner sensations.

Felt sense exercise: Follow my guidance below or, if you want to experience this exercise with my audio support, access the recording at DearGabby.com/HappyResources.

When practicing this method, try to focus only on the sensations rather than your thoughts. Even a few seconds of connection and presence are enough to allow the felt sense to come through.

Sit or lie down in a comfortable location where you have privacy and the ability to focus. Notice the sensations in your body. Is there a particular part of your body that reveals sensations to you? Describe the sensations. Take your time to open up to more and more subtle sensations and describe each one in detail.

Notice your feeling sensation.

Is there tension? If so, describe it. Is it dense, warm, inflamed, tight, rageful, sad?

Is there pressure? Describe it. Is it crushing, pounding, cutting off circulation?

Is there pain? If so, is it an ache, sharp, slight?

Does the sensation have a temperature? Is it cool, burning, on fire, icy?

Does the temperature have a color? Is it red, hot pink, or smoky?

Is there a texture? Is it soft, silky, rough?

Is there a weight? Heavy, light?

Is there a mood attached to the sense? Is it low, dark, uplifting?

Do you sense a taste of any kind? Sweet, bitter?

Is there a smell? Maybe you smell leaves or flowers.

Is there an absence or emptiness?

When you're ready, open your eyes and pick up your notebook. Describe any feelings that may have surfaced or any thoughts that came to mind. This exercise is about bringing awareness inside the body and slowing you down enough so that you notice your energetic, emotional, and sensory landscape. As you deepen the practice of connecting to the felt sense, you can begin to release chronic physical pain, have a better understanding of your true feelings, and enhance the efficacy of other therapeutic practices.

Recognizing the felt sense helps you connect to your feelings so that any unresolved ones can be processed.

Connecting to your body

There are several body-oriented practices I've used throughout my recovery. I turn to these practices whenever I notice myself feeling disconnected or uncomfortable. Each time I bring awareness to my body through movement, breath, and grounding exercises, I feel empowered knowing that I can bring myself back to peace. These practices are designed to make you more aware of the aliveness of your body and allow your physical energy to move in natural ways and not get stuck. Connecting to your body in this way will help your nervous system to regulate and release tension, leading to an inner peaceful state. I've experienced cathartic releases in as little as one minute after applying these methods.

1. **Move your body.** To release energy that gets locked up in your body, you can do either of these simple body-based practices as often as you wish. Even a short period of time can offer relief.

- **Grounded release:** Start by feeling your feet on the ground. Notice how the ground supports your feet. Then focus on how your feet support your ankles. Keep moving your focus up to your legs, hips, and spine, noticing how each part of you is connected to your feet and the ground. Next, lift your arms in the air on an inhale. On the exhale, swing your arms down and breathe out a sigh of relief. Let your knees move and your body move. Let your jaw relax and even jiggle as your mouth opens naturally. Repeat a few more times. Use this exercise to open the physical energy in your body.

- **Skip:** Skip around the room, the same way a child would skip freely, to move energy through your body. Afterward, stand still and allow your body to relax.

If you have physical limitations or pain conditions, try lying in bed and imagining your body moving in these ways. Visualization can be just as valuable, if not more, as actually moving because you have to focus on your inner sensations to visualize movement.

2. **Relax your tongue.** Another technique that helps your body relax is to allow your tongue to soften and relax onto the floor of your mouth. You'll notice that your breathing immediately becomes more gentle. When you notice that change in breath, say out loud to yourself, "I am alive, and I can breathe." I love this practice

and use it often. The moment I let my tongue soften, I automatically take a deep breath, feel my jaw relax, and become more connected to my body and emotions.

3. **Chant "Voooooo."** Chanting in any form can facilitate an inner sense of peace. When you open up to chant or sing and create a resonance in the lower belly, you stimulate your vagus nerve (responsible for regulating internal organ functions such as digestion, heart rate, and respiratory rate), which provides a signal to shut down an overstimulated nervous system. The vibration of chanting stimulates your vagus nerve, and making a *voooooo* sound enlivens the viscera (gut). The breath work helps you get centered in the present moment and a full expiration of breath produces a feeling of balance. When the vagus nerve is stimulated, your body gets the message that it's safe to relax, destress, release anxiety, and change your mood.

Do this practice in privacy so you don't limit your ability to fully embody the voo chant.

- Sit comfortably.
- Inhale slowly.
- Pause momentarily.
- On the out breath, make an extended *voooooo* sound, sustaining the sound throughout the entire exhalation. Vibrate the sound as if it were coming from your belly and focus on the

vibrations. Give yourself permission to make this sound as a full belly expression.

- At the end of the breath, pause briefly and allow the next breath to slowly fill your belly and chest again.

- When the in breath feels complete, pause and then make the *voooooo* sound again on the exhale until it feels complete.

- It's important to let the sound and breath expire fully before pausing. Let the next inhale come naturally. Don't force it. Repeat several times, then rest.

Focus your attention on your body, primarily on your abdomen, waiting and allowing your body to naturally adjust to the shift in your nervous system.

4. **Jin Shin Jyutsu hold.** Jin Shin Jyutsu is a Japanese healing modality thought to balance the body, mind, and spirit. This powerful practice can release tension, regulate arousal, and deepen relaxation. In short, it can help you feel safe.

   Practice either of the holds below for two to ten minutes:

   - **Head hold:** Place your right hand on your forehead and left hand on your heart. Breathe in deeply, and exhale completely. Look for a sensation of energy flow or relaxation.

- **Heart hold:** Place your right hand
  on your belly and left hand on your
  heart. Breathe in deeply, and exhale
  completely. Notice peace and relief set
  in. I use this hold when I'm meditating
  or before I go to sleep at night. When I
  was suffering with postpartum anxiety,
  this hold was my savior to calm my
  anxiety and connect to my body.

It's powerful to pray or affirm a sense of inner safety when you practice either of these holds. I love to say this prayer when I'm in a heart hold:

Thank you, angels, thank you, Spirit, for protecting me, guiding me, and keeping me safe.

The heart hold and this prayer bring me into an instant state of inner peace.

5. **Recall when you felt most like yourself.** This
   is another beautiful SE practice taught by Dr.
   Peter Levine. The practice aims to regulate
   the nervous system by reflecting when you
   previously felt most like yourself.

   - Take a moment to notice your overall
     experience.

   - Then recall a time in the last 24 hours
     when you felt most like yourself. (You
     can extend the time frame beyond 24
     hours if you need a larger window of
     reference.)

   - Allow yourself to recall the event with
     detail as if it were happening again. Pay

close attention to the five senses in this memory. Notice what happens in your body at this moment now.

- Next, recall another time in the past several weeks when you felt most like yourself or the person you'd like to be.

- Once again, allow yourself to recall the event with detail as if it were happening again. Pay close attention to the five senses in this memory. Notice what happens in your body at this moment now.

- What do you notice now about your overall experience?

This exercise allows you to get grounded in the felt sense in the present moment and in your adult resourced Self.

6. **Tapping.** In Chapter 6, I introduced the Emotional Freedom Techniques (EFT) of tapping. One simple tapping practice that you can apply anywhere at any time is to tap on the gamut point. The gamut point is located between the ring finger and the little finger, just below your last knuckles. Gently tap on the gamut point while breathing deeply and repeating to yourself, "I am safe. I am safe." This practice supported me early in my trauma recovery and throughout my postpartum anxiety and depression. Whenever I'd enter into a state of panic, I'd tap the gamut point with my mantra, "I am safe," until I calmed down.

7. **Meditate on a safe place.** By intentionally focusing on an imagined safe place, you can get out of a state of dissociation or avoidance. Follow the directions below or listen to my audible guidance at the resources link, DearGabby.com/HappyResources.

- Relax in a comfortable seated position.
- Gently close your eyes.
- Imagine a safe space. It can be a place you have been to before or it can come from your imagination.
- Notice how your body feels in the setting.
- What do you see?
- What do you hear?
- What do you smell?
- What do you feel?
- What do you taste?
- What can you touch?
- Allow yourself to imagine these five senses and ground your experience in the imagined place.

These simple practices empower you to care for your bodily sensations and regulate your nervous system in the moment, giving your body the ability to release stress and return to homeostasis.

A bridge back to presence

Like all the therapeutic practices I was drawn to, SE shared the same spiritual undertones. Getting out of my head and back into my body through SE practices was a way of releasing the stuck energy that had held me back from receiving inspiration, presence, and a greater connection to the energy of the Universe. For me, SE and other body-based practices have been a bridge back to presence. Through devotional practice, conscious awareness of my body, and consistent inquiry, I have grown to reconnect with my body, my physical sensations, and my ability to relish in the present moment. This healing process has offered me a beautiful connection to my inner felt sense and therefore a new sense of safety.

Initially I noticed my shift into the present moment while I was walking in the country. I started to notice sensations I'd never been present enough to take in. I noticed a profoundly joyful sense of gratitude for the nature around me. I noticed the freedom in my body. I noticed my jaw relaxed and my energy at peace. I noticed the chirping of the birds, the colors of the leaves, the sounds of nature around me. I noticed for the first time that I was truly present in the moment.

CHAPTER 9

Reparenting Yourself

"Peppa Pig, Peppa Pig, la la la la la la la la." The *Peppa Pig* jingle is on repeat in my head like a broken record. We're three months into the COVID-19 stay-at-home orders. My husband and I are running our business, managing our team, social distancing, and caregiving full time for a toddler. Like most parents during the first few months of the shutdown, we don't have childcare, so we do our best to toggle between Zoom calls and naptime. Our normally busy schedule feels ever more so with our boss (Oliver) calling the shots.

Even though so much uncertainty swirled around me, my internal condition had never been more steady. All the hard work in therapy was paying off. With my newfound baseline for safety and freedom, I was able to focus, be more present, and enjoy life's simple moments. Importantly, this was crucial for establishing a stronger bond with Oliver. For months, I'd carried the guilt that postpartum depression had gotten in the way of that precious bonding period between a mother and her baby. Now that I was feeling well, I knew it was the optimal time to strengthen my connection to my son and give him the presence, love, and security that every child deserves.

Guided toward deeper connection

My intention for deeper connection was enough for the Universe to step in and present me with clear direction. For months, a stack of parenting books had been resting on my nightstand. Then one night while meditating, my intuition said to me, "Read the book next to your bed!" Whenever I get these inspired hits toward teachers, books, and ideas, I know major guidance awaits. So without hesitation, I grabbed the book at the top of the pile: *The Power of Showing Up: How Parental Presence Shapes Who Our Kids Become and How Their Brains Get Wired* by Dr. Daniel Siegel and Tina Payne Bryson. I felt chills run down my spine as I opened the book. I always believe that whatever book lands in our lap is guided to us in the exact moment that we are ready to receive it. Spirit speaks to us through books, and authors become divine guides whether they realize it or not. So here I was, once again, presented with my own spiritual assignment in the exact moment when I could properly receive it. The book moved me so deeply that I think it should be required reading for any parent. The book helped me understand a child's brain wiring, its limitations, and the need for specific styles of nurturing in order to develop properly.

I had an amazing revelation as I explored Dr. Siegel's parenting techniques. At first I thought I was reading these books only to strengthen my bond with Oliver, but I came to see how I could apply them to myself. I could become my own internal parent and heal my past attachment wounds by respecting and honoring my inner child parts by applying the same methods I would offer to my son.

In order to establish a deeper connection with Ollie, I had to establish a deeper connection with myself, which meant looking more closely at the ways my past had shaped my present. When we lack security as children, we spend our adult lives searching for it in many ways outside ourselves—control, addiction, relationships, etc.—but what we really need is a newfound security that comes from within ourselves. We have the capacity to connect to Self (the parent within) to guide ourselves back to safety. (And if you are a parent, you can help your child develop a secure relationship with you because you can now show up for them by showing up for yourself first.)

Sometimes what we think we need to heal for others is exactly the healing we need for ourselves.

Parenting myself meant looking more closely at how my own childhood experience affected my inability to connect or feel safe in intimate relationships. I witnessed how I could never truly trust anyone to help me and how triggered I got when the people who were meant to care for me let me down. I explored all the ways the people in my life reacted when I was disconnected from the present moment. With love and compassion, I bravely witnessed the ways my unresolved childhood attachment wounds kept me from being present in my life and my relationships.

Neglect and trauma in my childhood led me to grow up with a disorganized attachment style. Dr. Siegel describes four types of attachment styles that occur in the parent-child relationship.[1] Understanding the attachment styles can help you see whether your childhood attachment, or lack thereof, plays a role in your life as an adult.

- **Optimal attachment** is when the parent is present and creates a secure environment for the child. At a young age, a child feels safe with the parent and experiences unconditional love. This doesn't mean that the parents are always perfect, but even when they get angry or fly off the handle, they can swiftly repair the situation by taking ownership of their own behavior and apologizing to the child. This helps the child learn that the intention behind the parent's actions is loving and compassionate no matter what. When a child witnesses a parent repair, the child's mirror neurons pick up one of the most important messages from the parent: It's possible to be human and still intend only love. (Dr. Siegel often refers to mirror neurons as sponge neurons because the child is literally sponging up what the parent is putting out.)

- **Avoidant attachment** occurs when a parent is unable to be present. This behavior can send a message to the child that the parent has no intention of connecting to them. The parent's inability to see or acknowledge the child's feelings creates a belief system that emotions do not exist and a sense of emptiness in the child that impacts development. They become unable to relate to their emotions, cut off from their own dreams, desires, intuition, and impulses. They are only able to focus on the physical and factual aspects of life.

- **Ambivalent attachment** occurs when a parent has unresolved anxiety and emotions. When a child experiences the parent's anxiety, the child can take on the same emotion. So if a parent shows up for a child's needs with anxiety, the child feels anxious about needing the parent. One day Mom or Dad can be reliable, and the next, they are stuck in their own anxiety and disconnected from the child. This leaves the child with insecurity because they sense that they cannot rely on their caregiver to be a steady source of security.

- **Disorganized attachment** is the most detrimental and occurs in the case of abuse or neglect. A child experiences disorganized attachment when the parent is the source of harm or fails to provide adequate safety. The child feels the intention to harm from the exact person who is supposed to protect them. In these instances, the brain becomes fragmented due to two conflicting responses: the natural biological response that leads a child toward the parent, and a signal from the brain warning that the parent is not safe. This can cause a child to literally walk toward a parent and immediately turn away or even fall to the ground and freeze. When a parent neglects or harms a child, it's often because of the parent's own unresolved trauma or grief. When a parent who experienced disorganized attachment as a child becomes a caregiver, they can unconsciously mirror that same behavior to their child, continuing the cycle.

As children, many of us did not foster a secure attachment with our primary caregivers because our core needs of being seen and secure were not met. Throughout our lives, we've been hiding or exiling the parts of ourselves that had unmet needs due to a breach in attachment. We've left those wounded inner child parts in the dark because we learned that they didn't matter or that they were shameful. That emotional denial didn't just go away. In fact, it has dictated the course of our lives. We've lived through the perceptual lens of our early attachment wounds, which can affect every area of life.

Learning to reparent myself

I could see how my commitment to transformational recovery would be the path to undoing the parenting patterns I experienced as a child. Dr. Siegel's work taught me that there was hope for rewiring my brain, my nervous system, and my relational attachment style. I no longer felt like the victim of my past; instead, I accepted that I could change my future. When we commit to therapeutic practices, unresolved states become resolved. Neuroplasticity (the ability of the brain to change) has the power to heal the adverse childhood experiences and the impact of trauma. Through awareness and therapeutic practices, we can reverse the consequences of suboptimal attachment and become safe.

Learning about attachment styles was another way for me to see myself through the lens of compassion. I could see how I was able to care for myself in the dark moments and guide myself to safety. I could have compassion for my protector parts. I could even see the Addict as a part of me who worked hard to protect me from the fear of unresolved traumatic emotions. When we learn to see ourselves through the lens of compassion, it frees us from our past and greatly benefits our own children or children we may care for.

We often look for safety outside
ourselves, but what we really need is
a newfound security that comes from
within ourselves and divine guidance.

Caring for the inner child parts

My devoted pursuit of feeling secure and living from Self
energy put me on a spiritual path of caring for the child parts
of myself in ways I'd never been cared for. I accepted that I
could be the leader in undoing the past so that I could live
the rest of my life safe, secure, and cared for in the present
moment. No partner, child, career accomplishment, friend,
or outside force could help me establish the secure attachment I longed for. It had to come from my own resourced
Self with the support of spiritual faith and a willingness to
grow. I welcomed spiritual guidance and asked the Universe
for support in the journey of reparenting myself.

Universal support showed up in Dr. Siegel's message that
secure attachment comes from establishing an environment
in which a child feels *safe, seen, soothed,* and *secure,* the Four
S's.[2] All that children need to grow up resilient and healthy
is to feel the presence of the Four S's in their developmental
years. The heartbreaking truth is that these primary needs of
a child are far too often unmet. When we grow up lacking the
security of the Four S's, we wind up searching for it in relationships, money, career credentials, or any outside source.
I knew it was imperative to make the Four S's my highest
parenting priority to help Oliver become a resilient, healthy
adult. Once again my commitment to Oliver became another
way the Universe guided me to care for my inner child.

Practice the Four S's with yourself

Helping my inner child parts feel safe, seen, soothed, and secure became a transformational practice that I now bring into every day of my life. I bring the same level of commitment to reparenting myself that I do for my son. As I made the Four S's a habit for my son, they became a habit for how I cared for myself. It became clear to me that my son was a powerful teacher for me on my healing path. Having a child helps us face the ways our inner child parts may not have received the optimal care they deserved. Facing that truth gives us the opportunity to provide that care for ourselves in a way we never received it. Now it's your turn to give yourself the security that you may have been missing in your childhood. Follow my guidance and let yourself relish in the endless stream of love that comes through.

Here's a breakdown of the Four S's and how to apply them to your own inner child. I encourage you to examine each of these areas and gently find ways to create an environment for yourself that helps you feel safe, seen, soothed, and secure. (And if you're a parent, I strongly encourage you to apply these practices with your children.)

Safe

We can't protect our children from every possible dangerous or adverse moment in life. But we can help them establish a sense of inner safety that will ultimately help them be resilient. Resilience provides one of the best chances for our children to live as healthy adults. This got me thinking about how I could help myself commit to living with a sense of safety, so I made a list.

How I've kept my inner child safe:

- Committing to weekly therapy sessions.

- Meditating for 40 minutes a day to regulate my nervous system and release stress.

- Advocating for myself in my work, with doctors, and in my relationships.

- Practicing sleep hygiene so that I could fall asleep and stay asleep throughout the night.

- Creating a home environment that felt comfortable and secure.

- Eating healthy food and taking supplements that made me feel confident in my ability to care for my body.

The list went on and on.

Taking note of all the ways I'd established a safe environment to live in helped me further commit. I made sure that I was anchoring each day with those practices. And whenever I'd notice myself out of alignment or feeling unsafe, I'd return to one of my self-care practices to reestablish an inner sense of safety. This practice is very empowering because it allowed me to stop relying on the outside to make me feel safe. In turn it showed me that I had the ability to restore a sense of inner safety without the need of an outside source.

If you feel called, make your own list now. How have you established safety in your life? If for some reason you can't think of anything, consider the fact that reading this book is an act of establishing a new baseline of safety.

Seen

"Truly seeing a child," says Dr. Siegel, "means we pay attention to his emotions—both positive and negative—and strive to attune to what's happening in his mind beneath his behavior."[3] Honoring a child's emotions, positive or negative, is one of the greatest gifts we can give them. But it's far too often that children grow up without being seen because their parents are unable to see their own emotions, let alone hold space for the child's big feelings.

I had spent most of my life trying to be seen, flaunting my accomplishments to anyone who would listen. But as I healed more, I outgrew that need. My newfound ability to honor my emotions and stay in tune with my spiritual connection gave me the greatest gift of all: the ability to care for myself because the person who mattered most finally saw me. I could see myself.

Truly seeing yourself doesn't happen overnight, especially if you grew up with an insecure attachment style. Don't let that hold you back; the past can be remedied by reparenting yourself in the present. You have the power to care for and acknowledge your emotions on a moment-to-moment basis. Your conscious awareness of your emotional reactivity, all of your parts and their extreme roles, and your desire to be seen is enough to start truly seeing yourself.

The past can be remedied by reparenting yourself in the present.

Here's how I began: I got curious about my emotional state rather than my reactive state. Whenever I noticed myself getting highly reactive, acting out, or feeling out of control, I knew that core emotions (inner child parts) needed respect and care. So instead of bulldozing past the emotions or shaming myself for how I reacted, I would ask myself a simple question, "What do you need to feel right now?" Then I gave myself permission to fully feel, honor, and respect whatever emotions came up. I let myself feel the rage, the anger, the frustration, the fear. I allowed myself to breathe into the space in my body where those emotions lived. And usually within a minute or so, I'd notice my energy shift, my ability to problem solve come back online, and my child parts were cared for. By simply giving myself permission to be with and honor my emotions through inquiry and breath, I was able to see all of myself. I've come to rely on this practice.

Try it out for yourself. The next time you notice yourself becoming reactive, stuck in an addictive pattern, or unconsciously emotional, ask yourself this, "What do you need to feel right now?" Don't judge the response that comes back. Give yourself permission to feel whatever comes up. Breathe into it, write it down, and honor your feelings. Unapologetically take time to truly see yourself and all of your big emotions. Give yourself the chance to be seen by you.

Soothed

When it comes to parenting, soothing isn't about doing everything for your child, it's about teaching your child that you will be there to help them show up for difficult experiences. Helping them know that they are not alone.

When it came to soothing my inner child parts, I intuitively turned to my spiritual practice. Throughout my life, I learned to rely on a spiritual connection as a way to soothe me in times of need and to know that I was never alone. I still need soothing from friends, therapists, and my husband. But I am not dependent on others to soothe me. I can turn to God (the Universe, or Spirit) to bring me the ease I long for. And as I learned more from IFS therapy, I realized that prayer and spiritual connection are a bridge back to my undamaged, resourced Self energy. Self is always there for me. I just need to turn to it for help. Some of the most profound moments of serenity have come through surrendering my protector parts to the care of Self. No matter how difficult the circumstances, I have access to spiritual and intuitive solutions through Self and the ever-present connection to love within me. Self is always there to show up and soothe the child parts.

The following meditation will help you feel soothed and connected to your own spiritual connection, your true nature, your Self. Follow the meditation below or go to DearGabby.com/HappyResources for my audio download.

Meditation for self-soothing

Sit comfortably in a chair with your feet planted firmly on the ground.

Roll your shoulders back and gently close your eyes.

Place your right hand on your heart and your left hand on your belly.

Notice any area in your body where you're experiencing any physical or emotional sensation.

Breathe into that space in your body, and on the exhale release.

As you breathe, honor all the feelings and emotions that come through.

Stay present with your feelings and emotions.

Breathe more deeply into the feelings, and on the exhale allow them to relax.

With each breath honor exactly how you feel.

Do not try to push anything away.

Become present with what needs to come through.

Allow your breath to become a source of soothing.

Breathe in deeply. Exhale completely.

Each breath becomes a gentle release and opportunity for relief.

Breathe in. Breathe out.

Continue this cycle of breath on your own.

Breathe into the feelings.

On the exhale release them.

Breathe into the feelings.

On the exhale release them.

Let your breath soothe you now.

When you're ready, open your eyes to the room.

Secure

When a child knows that they can consistently count on the parent to provide safety, opportunities to be seen, and soothing in times of need, that child will feel secure attachment. And that child is likely to thrive. Living the Four S's helped me establish an inner sense of security.

Even applying and committing to one of the Four S's will change the way you live. You'll no longer rely on other people to be your source of safety and security. You'll feel a sense of confidence and ease knowing that you are never alone and that you have the ability to care for yourself. Your relationships will grow and change because you'll let others off the hook, which will in turn give them permission to show up for you with more authenticity and less pressure. And you'll be able to care for and honor the children and loved ones in your life because you'll know what it truly means to care for yourself.

Take the Four S's to heart and give yourself the opportunity to parent yourself in a way that you never thought possible.

Establishing a strong connection with my own inner parent, the Self, has given me the security I always longed for. The best way I can describe this feeling is through an image. This image below shows a sketch on the cover of Richard Schwartz's latest book, *No Bad Parts*.

When I received the book in the mail, this image brought me to tears. The visual of a person holding themselves in an embrace reflected the inner safety I finally felt. The safety of knowing that at any moment I could turn to and rely on Self to lead me back to peace.

That sense of inner safety may feel far from reach, but I promise it's available to you. Don't underestimate the spiritual process that is occurring for you now. Opening up your conscious awareness to your own attachment wounds is an invitation for transformational healing. It's the first step in caring for your own inner child parts that have been hidden for so long. You've opened the door for intuitive guidance and Universal support. Practicing one of the Four S's is a radical act of self-care and can begin a journey of showing up for yourself in a way you never thought possible. Take that in and allow the inner transformation to unfold one miraculous step at a time.

To undo the past, we must become compassionate toward our present selves.

Let Self become the leader

With each day that went by focusing on my recovery, I became closer and more connected to Self. It became easier to witness my wounded child's coping mechanisms through the lens of love and respond to those triggered parts by applying one of the Four S's or other practices. Now when I'm triggered, instead of freaking out, I tune in to my body and emotions, and breathe into the feelings rather than running from them or pushing them away. I even wrap my arms around myself (like in the image from Schwartz's book cover) to give myself a hug. I have developed a toolbox of methods for self-regulation and connection to my own inner being.

In Chapter 7, you took the first step toward reparenting yourself. You began to recognize the ways you've been protecting yourself. And we introduced the idea of letting your adult resourced Self show up to support your child parts. The more we learn to rely on Self, the easier it becomes for the protectors to relax. When you establish a relationship to Self, you'll begin to intuitively know how to care for your protectors and therefore care for your inner exiled child parts that didn't receive healthy attachment. The more you strengthen your connection to Self, the easier it will be for Self to soothe them in the moment, which in turn helps them to let go of their extreme protective roles.

Connect to Self through meditation

This meditation will give you the beautiful opportunity of connecting to your undamaged, all-knowing Self—the inner parent that has always been there to help all of your parts coexist in harmony. Connecting to Self is a profound experience because it will give you a sense of safety and the belief that you can care for, support, and love yourself in any given moment. Follow along with the meditation guidance below, or visit DearGabby.com/HappyResources for my guided audio meditation.

In this IFS practice, I will encourage you to breathe, relax, and feel your heart.

- Close your eyes and take long, deep breaths. Allow your breath to regulate your nervous system and guide you into a parasympathetic relaxed state.

- Notice your diaphragm move naturally with each inhale and exhale.

- Breathe in deeply. Exhale completely.

- As you breathe, direct your focus inside and invite your body to relax a little bit.

- There's nowhere to go. Nothing to do. Just breathe.

- Identify any area of your body where there may be tension, and gently direct your breath into that space in your body.

- Breathe in, then on the exhale invite your body to let go.

- Now bring awareness to your heart. Breathe and focus on your heart.

- Pay attention to the inflow and outflow.

- With each breath, notice whether your heart feels open or closed. Allow your heart to open.

- As you breathe and create more space in your heart, notice whether you have any thoughts or feelings. Become aware of sensations in your body.

- Just notice. Notice who is there.

- Don't judge or attack what's happening inside.

- If you notice any parts that are judging your experience, gently ask them to relax and breathe.

- If you notice that you're being pulled away from yourself, that's fine. Just gently breathe and refocus on your inner awareness again.

- Continue breathing and feeling your heart. Continue to notice sensations, feelings, thoughts, and how you're feeling toward all of it.

- Feel what it's like to be with your Self.

If you feel inspired, pick up your pen and write about anything you noticed, how you're feeling now, and what that experience was like.

A prayer to connect to Self

Whenever I find myself disconnected from Self, I say a prayer to Self. The same way I intuitively pray to God, Spirit, Angels, or the Universe, I pray to Self. To me they are one and the same—an ever-present energy of love guiding my thoughts back to the present moment. Here are some examples of prayers to Self that have greatly benefited my life.

I welcome Self to care for all of my parts.

May Self energy support me in this moment.

May all parts be led by Self.

I surrender this extreme part to the care of Self.

I welcome Self to reorganize this for me.

May all parts feel love and accepted by Self.

Praying to Self is a divine practice of inviting Self energy into your consciousness to alchemize your triggered parts in the moment. Each time we turn to Self through prayer, we strengthen our connection. These prayers offer all of your parts the chance to calm down and be cared for.

Connect to Self in nature

I've found that a great way to connect to the energy of Self is in nature. If I'm struggling with work, or stuck in a protector part, I'll go for a walk outside. I will even go as far as to ask Self to take my protector parts for a walk to calm them down. While walking in nature I'll connect to my breath, ground my body, and allow the physical movement to clear the stagnant tension built up by my protectors. When I focus my attention on the blue sky or on taking in the fresh air, I experience the sensation of presence, thereby reconnecting to Self.

Try this out. The next time you notice yourself triggered by a protector part, take a walk outside, sit in the grass, go to a nearby park. Getting into nature will reconnect you with all of your senses, ground you back into your body, and realign you with the presence of the energy of Self that is always available to you.

When you let Self lead, you're showing your protectors and exiles that you are always there to support them no matter what. You learn to self-soothe in the moment and therefore establish a greater sense of security in your mind, body, and spirit. Self becomes the reliable parent who can show up for you whenever you feel unsafe or alone.

When you let Self lead, you're showing
your protectors and exiles that you are always
there to support them no matter what.

Self-regulating

These practices helped me respect my exiled inner child parts, whose emotions were neglected, denied, or ignored in some way. Little Gabby no longer had to show up in excessive ways to be seen and soothed. Whenever I felt uncared for, I could notice a protector part of me would begin to freak out, raise her voice, fight back, and try to gain some semblance of control, just like I did when I was a child. But now, instead of going into a full trigger response, I'd let Self speak to that part, "Thank you for your great work. You did a beautiful job protecting yourself. Now it's time to take a breath and let your child parts be cared for and brought back to safety." This simple inner dialogue between Self and my other parts gave me a great sense of inner strength and security. Rather than expecting myself to never be triggered again, to never act out, I instead allowed Self to show up and parent those triggered parts back to safety. This is the greatest practice of resilience.

The promise of resilience

Respecting a child's feelings is an act of respecting their brain development and their human condition. It's common for a parent to want to shush a child or say, "You're fine. You're okay." But when we shush and dismiss with our words or attitude, it's like saying, "Your feelings don't matter." Connection is key to helping a child feel worthy of their big emotions and preventing shame so that they become resilient.

The same goes for how we care for our inner child.

With the practices above, you're reparenting yourself and caring for every part of who you are. So the next time you feel triggered or notice a protector part take over, ask yourself the following questions:

- What do I need to feel safe right now?
- What do I need to feel seen right now?
- What do I need to feel soothed right now?
- What do I need to feel secure right now?

Between each question pause and allow your adult resourced Self to speak. Trust the inner guidance that you receive. This inquiry is a spiritual conversation between your inner child parts and your adult resourced Self. It's a form of prayer. Each time you connect to and care for your child parts, you strengthen your relationship with the inner wisdom of your resourced Self. Committing to this connection will help you establish the greatest relationship you'll ever know, the secure relationship to Self that you can always rely on. Developing this connection is like reclaiming the security you once lost as a child. Relying on your own inner parent will give you a newfound sense of safety and resilience to move through life with grace.

If you take five minutes to sit with these questions and get curious, you'll allow your protectors and child parts to speak up and be heard. You'll then be able to soothe them with compassion. That soothing will make you feel safe and secure. And in that state of security, your protectors can step back to let the Self lead. Once you notice that you're out of the triggered state and back in Self, you can then redirect.

But connection is required first. If you attempt to do this out of order, your child parts will only get more agitated, and your protectors will get louder.

Living these practices promises resilience. When faced with difficult situations, you'll know where to turn for support. When overwhelmed by life issues, you'll know how to calm yourself before you begin to problem solve. When activated in a relationship, you'll know how to deactivate the childhood triggers and get back to safety. Best of all, you'll know how to care for yourself in ways that you may have never experienced.

As I complete this chapter, Ollie is running around my office playing with my affirmation cards. I asked him to empty the box and put all the cards in the box. As he excitedly puts the cards back in the box, I notice him looking up at me. I say, "Ollie, would you like Mommy to read her book to you?" He responds, "Ya!" and continues boxing up his cards. As I read the words in this chapter, tears stream down my face. I recognize how grateful I am to have been able to show up for myself in all the ways I want to show up for him.

CHAPTER 10

Happy Days Ahead

I'm standing in the dark, eight feet above stage level. The theater is pitch black with only a spotlight fixed on my mouth as I utter disorganized sentences at a ferocious pace: " . . . *out . . . into this world . . . this world . . . tiny little thing . . . before its time . . . in a godfor– . . . what? . . . girl? . . . yes . . . tiny little girl . . . into this . . . out into this . . . before her time . . . godforsaken hole called . . . called . . . no matter . . . parents unknown . . . unheard of . . . he having vanished . . . thin air . . . no sooner buttoned up his breeches . . . she similarly . . . eight months later . . . almost to the tick . . . so no love . . . spared that . . . no love such as normally vented on the . . . speechless infant . . . in the home. . ."* and it goes on and on.

The audience is uncomfortable sitting in the darkness, assaulted by the speed of the voice, the vision of a mouth revealing emotions of terror, and what seems to be a confused story of suffering.

I was 18 years old when I chose to perform the absurdist play *Not I* by Samuel Beckett. The Mouth was a bizarre choice in roles for a young BFA theater student. For some reason, I was taken with the absurdist theater, especially this particular role. The only other light on the stage is a shadowy figure known as the Auditor, who makes four movements of "helpless compassion" whenever the Mouth is silent and seemingly listening to an inner voice. The Mouth's jumbled sentences represent the words of a 70-year-old woman who has been virtually mute since childhood with only occasional outbursts like this one portrayed onstage. The woman was born prematurely; her parents abandoned her at birth. The Mouth reveals her unspoken inner dialogue of a life frozen in the silence of her own suffering.

I didn't understand why I was drawn to this role, to the theater of the absurd, and to the work of Samuel Beckett. Not until now. Today I can see that the Mouth was speaking to me. She represented the silent suffering of trauma and the full expression of grief, rage, and terror. Giving voice to her suffering was the best I could do at that time to release my own. The drama, the focus, the voracious speed with which the Mouth moved, the violent nature of the language—it all felt like a cathartic release that I was unable to experience in my own life. My first attempt to discharge the pent-up energy of my own impermissible memories and suffering. My choice to study absurdist theater was a way of honoring an unknown shadowy side of myself, the place where my exiles lived.

Giving voice to her suffering was the best I could do at that time to release my own.

With decades of spiritual and personal growth behind me, I now understand why I felt so connected to the Mouth. I, too, felt silenced and shut down. I resonated with her inner dialogue of terror and the pressure of holding it down. I could feel her grief. I longed for the opportunity to speak my truth, relieve myself of the bondage of my past, and set myself free.

Touching into grief

When we experience a trauma (*big T* or *small t*), it's as if a part of our soul departs. There's a splitting off from a sense of safety into exiled parts filled with terror and fear. We become fragmented, frozen, and lost in the subconscious without a clear path out. I always felt this split; I just couldn't name it. It was far too scary to face the fact that an innocent part of myself had been so burdened.

When I was 27, I did a soul retrieval energy session with a shamanic healer. The session was designed to connect me to the child parts of myself that had been cut off. I remember the shaman saying that there was a little girl, around the age of five or six, and she was lost in a forest. The shaman explained that she saw this child filled with fear and terror. At the time, I had no recollection of what had happened in my past, but I felt the truth of her words deep within my body. I knew a part of me had been lost, but I was far from accepting that truth, let alone grieving it.

Grief is a deep emotion that we often don't feel safe enough to face. It lives beneath the shield of rage and in the shadow of heartbreak. It feels too painful to contemplate the grief of our past wounds.

We often consider grief an appropriate emotion only when we've experienced a socially acceptable loss such as the death of a loved one or a divorce. We're too ashamed or too unaware to give voice to the hidden grief that lingers in the shadows of our traumatic wounds. What we're afraid to accept is that our separation from safety, from peace, or from freedom was a loss in itself. It's a loss of innocence. That loss of a secure attachment, a peaceful childhood, a sense of inner safety. Those losses are hard to accept and hard to grieve.

Grief is difficult to uncover as it's buried beneath our protector parts such as rage, defensiveness, attack, judgment, shame, and other forms of outward projections. Before facing grief, we must recognize all the ways we've been running from it or fighting against it. This is a slow but necessary process. You can't rip the Band-Aid off too fast. Remember, our protectors have played an important role in our lives. They've kept us from being overwhelmed with feelings that we were not yet capable of handling. I can see clearly that my protectors worked tirelessly to keep me from ever having to experience grief.

As you read this, you may notice some resistance to the concept of grief. I didn't recognize it until I was 41 years old because I didn't feel I was even worthy of experiencing grief. Only now, as I write this chapter, am I finally able to acknowledge my own grief.

- The grief of living dissociated from my childhood.
- The grief of being disconnected from my body and afraid of everything.
- The grief of insecure attachments and the lack of security I deserved.

Today, though, I can face and honor the grief that I spent most of my life running from. Why now? Because I've gently peeled back the layers.

Respect what comes up

Contemplating the fact that you have something to grieve could activate a protector part of you. That part is likely going to show up as rage. In my experience, rage is present even if you don't notice it. Remember, from Chapter 4, when I introduced the work of Dr. Sarno and all the ways the pain in our bodies protects us from impermissible rage. Even if we don't identify as being rageful, it's there, hiding out in our back pain, our gastrointestinal issues, our TMJ, our headaches, and our anxiety. Rage shows up as a first responder to protect us from facing the truth of our grief. And if you did the Rage on the Page exercise in Chapter 4, you may have uncovered some grief.

Rage shows up as a first responder to protect us from facing the truth of our grief.

At 25, when I got sober, there was no way I could have contemplated all the loss. At 36, when I remembered the trauma, the shame and fear were way too extreme to consider the deeper emotion below them. And for the past five years, my rage and anger protected me from facing the heartbreaking truth of grief. Whenever my therapist had suggested that my rage was protecting me, I would go numb and dissociate. While I could intellectualize the concept, I hadn't been ready to face the deep emotions of grief. I shunned it because it would mean I'd have to face that I never felt lovable or good enough. My rageful protector part worked hard to keep me from ever having to face those truths.

So I lived in and out of episodes of protection. The protectors did their job, but it was time for them to stand down so that I could grieve once and for all. True relief from my suffering required that I become safe enough to express grief and give voice to my genuine experience.

Letting it out safely

Much like the character of the Mouth, we all hold down years of grief, mask it with rage, anesthetize it with addiction, and silence it. Grief from trauma, especially *big T* trauma, is like a pressure cooker. If we release it too fast, it becomes an uncontrollable outburst, which is what we unconsciously fear. Without realizing it, what we fear most is the possibility of who we could become when we let it out. In time, I could see that releasing grief meant I had to accept my past and the loss of my childhood innocence, the loss of a secure attachment, the loss of decades of living in fear, the loss of early bonding with my own son. I was terrified of who I'd become if all that grief came out at once.

We all hold down years of grief, mask it with rage, anesthetize it with addiction, and silence it.

Facing and releasing grief requires emotional resilience and inner safety. I had to have enough healing and connection to my adult resourced Self to take this big step. I had to be present, compassionate, and brave enough to witness the exiled emotions that had felt so threatened to be met in this way. Most of all, I had to trust that I was supported by my spiritual connection.

Grief starts with honoring the rageful protector parts for their great service and inviting them to step aside. Remember, all the ways we've been protecting ourselves are not bad. The protectors have kept us from an uncontrollable outburst of grief. But no one should live in that state forever. Letting it out has to be a slow and gentle process. A slow release.

Through the processes outlined in this book, I have become safe enough to let the protectors relax and step back while grieving the deeply wounded exiles. Each healing modality slowly allowed me to uncover this last emotion, this last action of grieving. Relying on the loving energy of Spirit to lead my healing journey, I was able to slowly titrate into the grieving process. *Titrate* is the operative word. While journaling, I'd experience moments of cathartic relief. In an hour of therapy, I may have had one minute of connection with grief. In yoga practice, I'd move stagnant energy through my body. Every therapeutic and spiritual practice had been perfectly planted into my life in the right time and order. With each day I'd peel back another layer of fear, getting closer to a safe place where I could finally grieve. One layer at a time, I've slowly, cautiously, and mindfully honored my wounds. I've allowed myself to be teachable, brave, and led by healing guidance so my resilience could grow.

Where Self comes in

In IFS when the therapist asks the patient how long they've been protecting their exiled parts, they commonly say, "Forever." It's likely that only now, after reading this book, you can even consider the idea that you've been protecting your exiled child parts from moving from the past into the present. In my work as a motivational speaker and on my podcast, *Dear Gabby*, I can see the same pattern in so many of the people I coach, no matter their issue: a protector part working really hard to silence the wounds of the past. From an addict struggling to get clean to a young woman suffering from a breakup, the same core wound keeps them stuck. The impermissible feelings of being unlovable, unsafe, unsupported, neglected, afraid, ashamed, and not good enough.

In a brief encounter with someone onstage or five minutes of coaching on the podcast, I can't save them, but I can guide them toward self-compassion and a connection to their adult resourced Self. I can help them see that their courage to get up in front of a live audience is their adult resourced Self and divine guidance showing up for them. Self has raised its hand, saying, "I need a miracle. I'm willing to change."

Your adult resourced Self has raised its hand, saying, "I need a miracle. I'm willing to change."

Self energy

In IFS, Self energy is our ability to feel safe in knowing all of our parts and holding them with love and compassion. Knowing our wounds, our patterns, our addictions, and our strengths. The more I connect to Self energy, the more steady I feel. Steady in the midst of a trigger, steady when things don't go my way, steady even when things are out of control. When I'm in alignment with Self energy, I feel inspired, wise, and accepting of what is. For years, I could access this energy only in fleeting moments. Today, I can tap into Self energy whenever I call upon it. In a recent conversation with IFS founder Richard Schwartz, I shared my experience of deepening my connection to Self energy. "It felt like eight years of hard IFS work for overnight Self energy," I said. He smiled at me as if he'd heard this countless times before.

While living with Self energy won't happen overnight, each method in this book has guided you to dismantle the wall you've built up against it. The metaphysical text *A Course in Miracles* says, "The course does not aim at teaching the meaning of love, for that is beyond what can be taught. It does aim, however, at removing the blocks to the awareness of love's presence, which is your natural inheritance."

Self (Love, God, Spirit, or whatever you choose to call it) has always been inside you, guiding you, supporting you, and awaiting your remembrance. You don't have to go out and find it or get to the perfect spiritual state to connect to it. All you need to do is stay committed one day at a time to healing and the presence of Self energy within you. Soon enough, you will become Self-led and able to grieve.

Melt away grief

When we begin the process of melting away our protection mechanisms and safely meeting what lives beneath them, that's when grief begins to melt away. We must heal the root-cause condition in order to become free. The root is grief. Our resistance to touching into grief keeps us frozen in time, as it's the driving force behind the way we react, respond, and protect ourselves. We must grieve our losses in order to come to peace with the absences and stolen pieces in our lives.

When we begin the process of melting away our protection mechanisms and safely meeting what lives beneath them, that's when we can truly heal.

When you are Self-led, you'll intuitively know the moments when it feels safe enough to grieve. One safe place to face your grief is in meditation. Sit comfortably and place your right hand on your heart and your left hand on your belly. With each breath become more and more present with the feelings that need to come forth. Breathe them in, and breathe them out. Meditating with your grief allows your protector parts to calm down, thereby letting Self step in.

When you feel ready, I suggest you start by acknowledging the losses you've faced. Gently consider the following questions. Maybe write about them in your journal, or bring them up in a therapy session.

- Look back at the feelings associated with your triggers from Chapter 2. What do those feelings or deeper impermissible feelings reveal about what you lost? For instance, if you feel afraid, you may have lost a sense of safety. If you feel anxious, you may have lost a sense of peace. If you feel unlovable, you may have lost confidence that you are lovable and loved.

- What parts of your life, your body, or your mind were interrupted or changed?

- What dreams or future plans never came to be as a direct result of your trauma?

Give voice to the grief so you can heal it and find inner peace. You've already faced so many challenging emotions; don't let yourself be afraid of this one. Whatever comes, honor how the grief shows up and let it move through you. Since the grief has been buried deeply, truly allowing yourself to grieve is the final step to accepting and forgiving your past so you can experience true peace and freedom in the present. As you gently move through grief, make sure to reach out for guidance from others too. Seek therapeutic counsel, support from a loved one, or listen to any of my meditations at DearGabby.com/HappyResources to feel my presence guiding you.

Knowing that someone is rooting for your recovery is imperative. The people who land in our lives to support our growth are human angels. The therapists, yoga teachers, coaches, authors, and even strangers who smile at us on the street are divinely planted on our path. They come to us to help us remember we're not alone in our suffering and that someone cares. I want you to feel that love from me right now. I want you to know I care about your recovery, and I'm proud of you.

Love is what we want most, but often we resist it. We resist it because it can feel far too vulnerable to trust that someone truly cares about us. But it's imperative to our healing journey that we allow ourselves to be seen—first by seeing ourselves and loving ourselves. Then we open up to others. When we show our truth, respect our shame, and honor our wounds, we become liberated. The moment we reveal our true feelings to another human, we offer up a gift. It's a gift to allow yourself to be seen. When someone is let in on your truth, you even give them permission to identify their own.

It's imperative to our healing journey that we allow ourselves to be truly seen by first seeing ourselves and loving ourselves.

When freedom sets in

Once I had the courage to grieve, it became easier to feel safe in my mind and my body. Facing the truth of grief set me free because I no longer had to run from the fear of reliving that pain. By welcoming the feeling and honoring my past, I became safe. I no longer had to run from the fear of my feelings; instead, I could accept every part of me. That acceptance cleared the path for the light of love to enter me.

Sometimes safety sets in when we least expect it. The other day I was receiving treatment for my TMJ. At this point, the TMJ felt like my final frontier, a subconscious last-ditch effort to hold on to a false sense of security. I sought support from my local osteopath. I lay facing upward on the table as he gently placed light pressure around my neck, shoulders, back, and then upward toward my jaw. As he pressed into my jaw, he said, "Hold a vision of a sun at the center of your chest. Let the sun shine brightly and allow it to expand from the inside out." Then he repeated this phrase several times: "Absolute faith and trust."

As he repeated that phrase, an image came into my mind. I saw myself floating in a vast open ocean. There was nothing around me. I was floating with nowhere to go. The water was still, and the sun felt warm on my face and body. I took a deep breath and relaxed. Then I saw a vision of a large hand underneath my body holding me up in the water. I no longer had to rely on the buoyancy of the ocean to keep me afloat or be concerned about the waves picking up. I was held like a baby in the palm of a hand. I allowed myself to lean deeper and deeper into this vision. Intuitively I knew that this image resembled the hand of a Higher Power keeping me safe, secure, and protected.

As I held the vision, a sense of safety settled into my entire body. My heart opened, my nervous system relaxed, and my jaw released. I heard a clicking in my jaw as the tension melted away. I was no longer holding on. I was no longer protecting myself. I was held. I was safe. I was finally free.

I can look back now and see how there were no accidents along the way. The decades of healing unfolded just as they were supposed to.

Amma, the hugging saint, said, "When an eggshell cracks from the outside it's broken, when it cracks from the inside it's reborn." My prayer is that this book has cracked you open to your innocence, your true love nature, and the hidden parts of you that have longed to be set free. I hope you feel a sense of safety knowing that there is a way out of suffering, there is a path to peace, there are people ready to support your healing, and there is a spiritual presence of love guiding you every step of the way.

I believe in you

Don't underestimate the subtle shifts you've made in the course of this work. You didn't give up; you didn't run. You stayed steady, willing, and receptive in the midst of triggers, tough truths, and fear. Your adult resourced Self and divine guidance have led you here. It doesn't matter if you haven't changed your patterns by this point, or if you still feel like you're stuck or suffering. That's okay. What matters is that you've been brave enough to wonder what lives beneath your patterns and you've let Self lead you through moments of truth and radical acceptance. Your curiosity about these methods, your willingness to keep reading, your acceptance of yourself, the brief encounter with a truthful feeling— these are all enough to get you closer to the truth of who you are. The subtle shifts will add up, and one day you'll wake up new.

In these pages I've vulnerably shared my truth in hopes that I will help you know you're not alone. My passion for spirituality and personal growth led me on the exploratory journey that I shared here. I don't expect your path to look like mine, but I pray that this book inspires you to practice one or more of these methods so you can feel empowered on your journey toward inner freedom. My prayer is that this book inspires your own Self-guided path to recovery from the past.

As I write this chapter, I feel so proud of you that a surge of energy is moving through my hands as I type. I'm proud of your bravery, your commitment to freedom, and your willingness to grow. I'm proud of you for opening this book in the first place. I'm proud that you've made it this far. Life can be hard, but recovery is miraculous. Each step of the recovery process is a miracle. An aha moment while reading this book is a miracle. A brief encounter with your resourced Self is a miracle. The cathartic ugly cry on the sofa is a miracle. The bravery to ask for help is a miracle. You, my friend, are a miracle!

I have often felt like a spiritual midwife, here to guide you through the journey of being reborn. I trust in you and your ability to heal, no matter how big or small the trauma has been in your life. I can't see you in your past; I see you only as your whole resourced Self in this present moment. No matter how horrific your past may have been, I believe in you. If no one has ever said that to you before, it may be hard to take that in.

Maybe it's hard to believe that I could care about a stranger. I get it. It's hard to accept that someone could believe in your healing and your ability to be free. It's hard to consider that someone understands your pain. While I may feel like a distant author whom you may never meet in person, please don't underestimate the energy exchange that's happening here. Each word in this book is infused with my intention to help you know that you're not alone. Even if our stories are drastically different, I expect that at some point you've recognized yourself in me. That's because we all suffer. We all have experiences that cause us pain. And we all have the same source of love within us ready to show up the moment we remember it's there. That's why I can write these words with genuine truth: I see you.

My intention is for the energy of love pouring through me now to permeate your being. I want you to feel the transmission of pride coming through this page. I want you to know I'm rooting for you every step of the way. I want you to know you are seen and you are loved. Most important, God, the Universe, Spirit guides, and the ever-present Self energy of love are within you and around you every step of the way. Allow your Self to enter into that love right now.

- Gently place your right hand on your heart and your left hand on your belly.

- Take a deep breath in. And let it go.

- On the next inhale, allow your diaphragm to extend; on the exhale, let it relax.

- Breathe in, and breathe out.

- Say to yourself, *I am cared for, I am loved.*

Now, sit silently for a moment with your eyes closed and feel my energy, my compassion, my understanding, my faith, and my love for you. Trust that the energy I'm infusing into these words has the power to come off the page. Give yourself permission to accept that someone in the world cares deeply about you. Someone understands your suffering and believes you can recover. Someone knows you are on your way to peace and freedom. Give yourself permission to believe it too and welcome the Happy Days ahead.

RESOURCES

As I said at the start of this book, the work you've begun here is a journey toward lifelong transformation. So I've gathered some information to support you on your journey beyond these pages.

If what you've read has triggered painful feelings . . . if you're dealing with the effects of big-T or small-t trauma in your own life . . . or if you simply want to delve deeper . . . these resources can help you learn more about the practices we've discussed, use the insights you've gained, or connect with a professional to guide you in your healing work.

Please visit DearGabby.com/HappyResources for tools you can carry forward on your path of unlearning fear and remembering love.

ENDNOTES

Chapter 1

1. Regina M. Sullivan, "The Neurobiology of Attachment to Nurturing and Abusive Caregivers," *Hastings Law Journal* 63, no. 6 (August 2012):1553–1570. https://www.ncbi.nlm.nih.gov/pmc/articles/PMC3774302/.

2. Thich Nhat Hanh, *No Mud, No Lotus* (Berkeley, CA: Parallax Press, 2014).

Chapter 3

1. Helen Schucman, *A Course in Miracles* (New York: Viking: The Foundation for Inner Peace, 1976), W-p1.153.

2. Ibid., T-1.I.11.

Chapter 4

1. John E. Sarno, *Healing Back Pain: The Mind-Body Connection* (New York: Grand Central Publishing, 1991).

2. Richard N. Forgoros, "Anatomy of the Vagus Nerve," verywellhealth.com, last modified June 17, 2020. https://www.verywellhealth.com/vagus-nerve-anatomy-1746123.

3. Helen Schucman, *A Course in Miracles Workbook for Students* (New York: Viking: The Foundation for Inner Peace, 1976), W-p1.199.

Chapter 5

1. E. Tronick, et al., "Infant Emotions in Normal and Pertubated Interactions," paper presented at the biennial meeting of the Society for Research in Child Development, Denver, CO, April 1975. Also see Jason G. Goldman, "Ed Tronick and the 'Still Face Experiment,'" *Scientific American*, October 18, 2010.

2. Dana R. Carney, Amy J. C. Cuddy, and Andy J. Yap, "Power Posing: Brief Nonverbal Displays Affect Neuroendocrine Levels and Risk Tolerance," *Psychological Science* 21, no. 10 (October 2010):1363–1368. https://doi.org/10.1177/0956797610383437.

Chapter 6

1. "Conditioned Reflexes and Neuron Organization," *JAMA* 139, no. 15 (April 1949):1045. doi:10.1001/jama.1949.02900320075040. Also see Melanie Greenberg, "Understanding the Trauma Brain," *Psychology Today*, last modified June 30, 2021. https://www.psychologytoday.com/us/blog/the-mindful-self-express/202106/understanding-the-trauma-brain.

2. Schucman, *A Course in Miracles*, T-14.VI.1.

Chapter 7

1. Schucman, *A Course in Miracles*, T-10.IV.8.

Chapter 8

1. Peter A. Levine, *In an Unspoken Voice: How the Body Releases Trauma and Restores Goodness* (Berkeley, CA: North Atlantic Books, 2010).

2. "Peter Levine on Somatic Experiencing," interview by Marie-Helene Yalom and Victor Yalom, Psychotherapy.net, (April 2010). https://www.psychotherapy.net/interview/interview-peter-levine.

3. Peter A. Levine, "Somatic Experiencing," Ergos Institute of Somatic Education, https://www.somaticexperiencing.com/somatic-experiencing.

4. Bessel van der Kolk, *The Body Keeps the Score: Brain, Mind, and Body in the Healing of Trauma* (New York: Viking Press, 2014).

Chapter 9

1. Daniel J. Siegel, "How We Attach: Relationships between Parents and Children," chap.5 in *Parenting from the Inside Out: How a Deeper Self-Understanding Can Help You Raise Children Who Thrive* (New York: TarcherPerigee, 2003).

2. Daniel J. Siegel and Tina Payne Bryson, *The Power of Showing Up: How Parental Presence Shapes Who Our Kids Become and How Their Brains Get Wired* (New York: Ballantine, 2020).

3. Siegel and Bryson, *The Power of Showing Up*.

INDEX

Page numbers in *italics* reference figures.

A

AA. *See* Alcoholics Anonymous
Addiction
  author's personal experience, 1–3,
    11–12, 25–33, 46
  author's words of guidance,
    35–36, 43
  breathwork for, 41–42
  causes of, 26–27, 33–35, 46, 49–51
  grief and, 202–203
  as hypervigilance response, 52
  Internal Family Systems (IFS)
    therapy and, 148
  "Me too," 132–133
  as protection, 140, 147–148
  reparenting yourself and, 177
  shame and, 103, 132–133
  spiritual guidance for, 42–43
  stigma of, 132–133
  toll of, 29–32, 148
  trigger and pattern identification,
    37–40, 61
  types of, 25–30, 100–101
Affirmations, 88–90, 91, 110–111
Alcoholics Anonymous (AA), 61,
  131, 132–133, 148
Amygdala, 51–52, 58, 122, 127. *See
  also* Fear and fear response
Angelou, Maya, 146
Antidepressant medication,
  114–123
Attachment breaches
  author's personal experience, 88,
    95–97, 98
  background, 9

IFS for, 140
influence of, 34–35
reparenting and, 176–180. *See also*
  Reparenting yourself
shame and, 96–99, 100–104
Attachment styles, 9, 178–180

B

Back pain, 74–75, 80–81, 87, 201
Beckett, Samuel, 197–198
Bilateral music, 83, 85–86
Bilateral stimulation, 123–124
Binge eating, 140–141
Biology. *See* Neurobiology
Body identification, 78–80
The Body Keeps the Score (van der
  Kolk), 164–165
Brain. *See* Amygdala; Mind-body
  connection; Neurobiology
Brand, Russell, 147–148
Breathwork, 41–42, 63, 151, 158
Bryson, Tina Payne, 176

C

Chanting, 169–170
Childhood trauma and neglect. *See*
  Attachment breaches; Repar-
  enting yourself; Sexual abuse;
  Trauma healing
Codependency, 25–26, 33, 100–101
Compassion. *See* Self-compassion
Coping mechanisms, 25–28,
  59–60. *See also* Addiction; Fight
  response; Flight response; Freeze
  response

A Course in Miracles (metaphysical text), 60, 63, 78, 131, 149, 205

COVID-19 pandemic, 12, 22–23, 58, 142, 175

D

Depression. *See also* Postpartum depression
antidepressants for, 114–123
author's personal experience, 113–118, 133–134
EFT for, 126–130
EMDR for, 123–125
neurology of, 121–123
speak your truth, 131–132
stigma of, 118–123
suffering alone, 132–134

Dissociation and dissociated memories
author's personal experience, 45–48, 51, 53, 124–125, 135–136
fear and, 59–60
neurobiology of, 51–54, 58, 104–105
protector parts and, 135–136. *See also* Protector parts
PTSD and, 164
transformational trauma healing therapies for, 123–128. *See also* EFT; EMDR
as trauma symptom, 45–48, 50–51
triggers for, 53, 57–58

E

EFT (Emotional Freedom Techniques)
author's personal experience, 49
background, 73, 126–128, *127*
felt sense exercise, 172
journaling and, 131
shame exercise, 128–130

EMDR (Eye Movement Desensitization and Reprocessing)
author's personal experience, 49, 73

background, 73, 123–125, 164–165
spiritual guidance system and, 125
window of tolerance and, 118

Emotional Freedom Techniques. *See* EFT

Energy meridians, 126–128, *127*

Exiled parts, 138–141, 142, 152, 156–157, 203–204

Eye Movement Desensitization and Reprocessing. *See* EMDR

F

Fear and fear response
background, 59–60
interruption of, 61–67
self-forgiveness and, 150
therapies for, 127, 149
triggers, 61

Felt sense exercises, 165–167, 172

Fight response
journaling and, 82–86
neurobiology of, 76–77, 161
protector parts and, 13
triggers for, 33–35, 37–38

"Flawsome," 110

Flight response
breathwork for, 41–42
coping mechanisms for, 26–30, 34
dissociation and, 46–69. *See also* Dissociation and dissociated memories
grief and, 200
interrupting, 61–69
neurology of, 53–54, 58, 59–60, 161
protector parts and, 138, 140
shame and, 95–96
triggers for, 33–40

Four S's (safe, seen, soothed, and secure), 181, 182–189

Freeze response
author's personal experience, 159–160, 174

body-oriented practices for, 160–163, 167–173, 174
dissociated memories and, 45–46
felt sense, 164–167
grief and, 199–200, 205
neurology of, 51–52, 53–54, 161–162
shame and, 104–106

G

Gastrointestinal issues, 30, 54, 71–73, 76–78, 201
Grief
    author's personal experience, 197–198, 199, 201, 208–209
    author's words of guidance, 209–211
    background, 199–200
    freedom from, 208–209
    letting it out safely, 201, 202–203, 205–207
    rage and, 200–201
    Self connection for, 203–204, 206
    Self energy and, 204–205
Grounded release, 168
"Ground your body" pose, 109–110

H

"Happy Days!" xviii–xix, 209–211. *See also* Inner peace journey
Hay, Louise, 71, 88–89
Healing from trauma. *See* Trauma healing
Hicks, Abraham, 7
Hypervigilance, 52, 104, 121–122, 164

I

IFS. *See* Internal Family Systems (IFS) therapy
In an Unspoken Voice (Levine), 160–161
Inner child parts
    care for, 157, 181–189

as exiled part, 139
reparenting and, 175–196. *See also* Reparenting yourself
Inner peace journey
    author's words of guidance, 13–14
    coping mechanisms, 1–3, 11–13, 25–28, 59–60. *See also* Addiction; Fight response; Flight response; Freeze response; Protector parts
    free will and, 1–3
    honor the suffering, 17–18
    "protector" parts and, 12–14. *See also* Protector parts
    spirituality and, 5–6, 15–16, 21–22. *See also* Spiritual guidance system
    surrendering, one step at a time, 22–24. *See also* Trauma healing
    symptoms of unhealed trauma, 7–11. *See also* Depression; Freeze response; Grief; Psychosomatic conditions; Shame
    vision for, 4–6, 18–22
    worthiness and, 6–7
Insomnia, 54, 77, 113–117, 157–158
Internal Family Systems (IFS) therapy
    for addiction, 148
    author's personal experience, 142, 144–145, 157–158
    background, 137–141, 137n
    benefits of, 155–157
    grief and, 203–204
    meditation practice for Self connection, 190–192
    Self connection and, 137n, 143–146, 150, 190–192
    Self energy and, 204–205
    self practice, 152–154
    spiritual guidance system and, 149–151

J

Jin Shin Jyutsu hold, 170–171

Journaling
author's personal experience, 2–3, 87–88, 203
for fear response interruption, 62
on grief, 201, 203, 206
on protector parts, 153–154
Rage on the Page practice, 82–88, 201
for shame awareness, 106–107
speak your truth through, 131–132
trigger identification through, 37–39, 88
on vision for new life, 19
"Journal Speak," 83

L

Levine, Peter, 160–161, 165, 171–172

M

Mahan, Brian, 102, 104, 110
Meditation
freeze response and, 173
grief and, 206–207
positive affirmations and, 88–90, 91, 110–111
protector parts and, 153–154
Rage on the Page practice, 85–86
Self connection through, 190–192
for self-soothing, 186–187
Memories. *See* Dissociation and dissociated memories
Meridians, 126–128, *127*
"Me too," 49, 94, 132–133
Mind-body connection, 71–91
affirmations for, 88–90, 91
author's personal experience, 71–73
background, 73–75
body identification, 78–79
Rage on the Page practice, 82–88, 201
releasing negative emotions, 87

spiritual relationship to your body, 79–80
stress and, 80–81
subconscious support, 87–88
sympathetic overdrive, 76–78
talking back to your brain, 81–82
Miracles, as shift in perception, 63–64
Mouth role, from *Not I* play, 197–198, 202

N

Nature, 193
Neurobiology
of depression, 121–123
of dissociated memories, 51–54, 58, 104–105
of fight response, 76–78, 161
of flight response, 53–54, 58, 59–60, 161
of freeze response, 51–52, 53–54, 161–162
of shame, 98–99, 104–105
of tapping (EFT), 127
window of tolerance, 118
Nhat Hanh, Thich, 17
No Bad Parts (Schwartz), 188
Not I (Beckett), 197–198
Numbness. *See* Dissociation and dissociated memories; Freeze response

O

Optimal attachment, 178

P

Parasympathetic state, 76
Parenting. *See* Reparenting yourself
Physical symptoms. *See* Mind-body connection; Psychosomatic conditions; *specific symptoms*
Physiology. *See* Neurobiology
The Polyvagal Theory (Porges), 104–105

Porges, Stephen, 104–105

Positive affirmations, 88–90, 91, 110–111

Postpartum depression
antidepressants for, 114–117, 120–122
author's personal experience, 113–118, 133–134
neurobiology of, 122–123

Post-traumatic stress disorder (PTSD), 94, 126, 164. *See also* Fight response; Flight response; Freeze response

The Power of Showing Up (Siegel & Bryson), 176

Power pose, 109

Prayer
for acceptance and guidance, 14, 16, 21–22, 32–33, 42–43, 68–69
for honoring shame, 106, 111
for Jin Shin Jyutsu hold, 171
for mind-body connection, 80
for relief, 56, 63–64
for Self connection, 150–151, 192, 195
for self-soothing, 185–186
truth acknowledgement as, 131–132

Protector parts
author's personal experience, 135–136, 142, 144–147, 156–158
background, 12–14
grief and, 202–203
honoring, 146–148, 150–151, 152–157
IFS on, 137–157. *See also* Internal Family Systems (IFS) therapy
spiritual guidance system for, 149–151

Psychosomatic conditions
author's personal experience, 54, 71–73, 76
author's words of guidance, 90–91
background, 73–75

body identification and, 78–81
body shift and, 87
spiritual guidance system for, 55–56, 75, 78–80
subconscious emotions and, 81–86
sympathetic overdrive, 76–78, 161
talking back to your brain, 81–82

PTSD. *See* Post-traumatic stress disorder

R

Rage, 50–51, 74, 140, 199–202. *See also* Fight response

Rage on the Page practice, 82–88, 201

Reparenting yourself, 175–196
author's personal experience, 175, 180, 194
background, 176–180
Four S's and, 181, 182–189
inner child care, 157, 181–189
melting away, 205–207
resilience through, 194–196
Self and, 137n, 143–146, 177. *See also* Self

Repressed memories. *See* Dissociation and dissociated memories

Resilience, 194–196

Romantic codependency, 25–26, 33, 100–101

Running. *See* Flight response

S

Sachs, Nicole, 82–83

Sarno, John, 73–75, 78–83, 201

Schwartz, Richard, 137, 137n, 146, 152, 188, 204

SE (Somatic Experiencing), 159, 160–164, 171–172, 174

Secure attachments, 9, 187–189. *See also* Four S's

Self
background, 137n, 143–146, 177

connecting to, 151, 156–158, 172, 177, 190–193, 195
Four S's and, 186, 188–189
grief and, 203–204, 206
IFS therapy and, 137n, 143–146, 150, 190–192
prayer for, 150–151, 190–192, 195
qualities of, 143
regulation of, 189–190, 194
resilience and, 194–196
Self energy, 204–205, 211
spiritual guidance system and, 150–151
Self-compassion
author's personal experience, 121–122
grief and, 204
Internal Family Systems (IFS) therapy and, 150
protector parts and, 152–153, 155
shame and, 110–111, 117
Self energy, 204–205, 211
Self-soothing, 185–187
Sexual abuse
author's choice of survival, 49–50, 66–67. *See also* Trauma healing
author's dissociated memory of, 45–48, 93–94
"Me too," 49, 94
Shame
acceptance of, 98–99, 107–108
anti-depressant use and, 115–116, 118–123
author's personal experience, 93–97, 132, 133
author's words of guidance, 132–133, 134
avoidance mechanisms, 100–104
awareness practices, 106–107
depression and, 118–123
EFT for, 128–130
fear response and, 64–65
neurological response to, 98–99, 104–105
origins of, 97–98

resources for facing, 108–112, 117
speak your truth, 131–132
suffering alone, 132–134
triggers, 98, 105–108
Siegel, Daniel, 118, 176, 177–179, 183–184
Singer, Michael, 23
Skipping (movement), 168
Sleep deprivation, 54, 77, 113–117, 157–158
Somatic Experiencing. *See* SE
Soul retrieval energy session, 199
Spiritual guidance system. *See also* Prayer; Self
for addiction, 42–43
author's words of guidance, xviii
background, 5–6, 15–16, 21–22
brain rewiring and, 123
Internal Family Systems (IFS) therapy and, 149–151
Somatic Experiencing and, 174
transformational trauma healing therapies and, 125, 126
for trauma healing, 55–56, 66–69
Still Face Experiment, 98
Stress response
affirmations and, 88–90, 91
author's words of guidance, 90–91
mind-body connection, 80–81
sympathetic overdrive, 76–78
symptoms of, 51–52, 72–75, 77
Superman pose, 109
Sympathetic overdrive, 76–78, 104
Symptoms. *See* Psychosomatic conditions; *specific symptoms*

T

Tapping. *See* EFT
Tension myoneural syndrome (TMS), 74
Temporomandibular joint syndrome (TMJ), 30, 54, 83, 201, 208–209

Tongue relaxation, 168–169

Transformational trauma healing therapies, 117–118, 124–126. *See also* EFT; EMDR

Trauma healing. *See also* Reparenting yourself

author's personal experience, 45–50, 71–73

awareness as catalyst for recovery, 57–58

big T trauma, 8–10, 52, 53, 202

effects of, 50–52

fear response and, 59–67. *See also* Fear and fear response

self-regulation techniques, 126. *See also* EFT

shame and, 93–112

small t trauma, 8–10, 52, 58

spiritual guidance system for, 55–56, 66–69

symptoms of unhealed trauma, 71–91. *See also* Depression; Dissociation and dissociated memories; Freeze response; Grief; Psychosomatic conditions; Shame

therapies. *See* EFT; EMDR; Internal Family Systems (IFS) therapy; Somatic Experiencing (SE)

Triggers. *See also* Reparenting yourself

for addiction, 37–40, 61

body identification and, 79–80

for dissociated memories, 53, 57–58

of fear response, 61

identification through journaling, 37–39, 88

IFS for, 138–141

public admission of trauma as, 94

responses to, 64–65

of shame, 98, 105–108

Tronick, Edward, 98–99

12-step programs, 12, 61, 131, 132–133, 148

U

Under the Skin (podcast), 147–148

V

Van der Kolk, Bessel, 164–165

Vulnerability

author's personal experience, xvii, 30–32, 95

author's words of guidance, xvii–xviii

"Me too," 94

W

Window of tolerance, 118

Winfrey, Oprah, 28

Wonder Woman pose, 109

Work addiction, 26, 28–30

Writing. *See* Journaling

Y

You Can Heal Your Life (Hay), 71

ABOUT THE
AUTHOR

For more than 16 years, Gabby Bernstein has been transforming lives—including her own. The #1 *New York Times* best-selling author has penned nine books, including *The Universe Has Your Back* and *Super Attractor*. Gabby was featured on Oprah's *Super Soul Sunday* as a "next-generation thought leader." *The New York Times* identified Gabby as "a new role model." In her weekly podcast, *Dear Gabby*, she offers up real-time coaching, straight talk, and conversations about personal growth and spirituality. From her start hosting intimate conversations with 20 people in her New York City apartment, Gabby has grown to speaking to tens of thousands in sold-out venues throughout the world. For more, visit gabbybernstein.com.

Hay House Titles of Related Interest

YOU CAN HEAL YOUR LIFE, the movie, starring
Louise Hay & Friends
(available as an online streaming video)
www.hayhouse.com/louise-movie

THE SHIFT, the movie,
starring Dr. Wayne W. Dyer
(available as an online streaming video)
www.hayhouse.com/the-shift-movie

***

*SUPER ATTRACTOR: Methods for Manifesting a Life
beyond Your Wildest Dreams*

THE UNIVERSE HAS YOUR BACK: Transform Fear to Faith

*MIRACLES NOW: 108 Life-Changing Tools for Less Stress,
More Flow, and Finding Your True Purpose*

SUPER ATTRACTOR: A 52-Card Deck

THE UNIVERSE HAS YOUR BACK: A 52-Card Deck

MIRACLES NOW: A 62-Card Deck

All of the above are available at your local bookstore,
or may be ordered by contacting Hay House (see next page).

***

We hope you enjoyed this Hay House book. If you'd like to receive our online catalog featuring additional information on Hay House books and products, or if you'd like to find out more about the Hay Foundation, please contact:

Hay House, Inc., P.O. Box 5100, Carlsbad, CA 92018-5100
(760) 431-7695 or (800) 654-5126
(760) 431-6948 (fax) or (800) 650-5115 (fax)
www.hayhouse.com® • www.hayfoundation.org

———

Published in Australia by: Hay House Australia Pty. Ltd.,
18/36 Ralph St., Alexandria NSW 2015
Phone: 612-9669-4299 • *Fax:* 612-9669-4144
www.hayhouse.com.au

Published in the United Kingdom by: Hay House UK, Ltd.,
The Sixth Floor, Watson House, 54 Baker Street, London W1U 7BU
Phone: +44 (0)20 3927 7290 • *Fax:* +44 (0)20 3927 7291
www.hayhouse.co.uk

Published in India by: Hay House Publishers India,
Muskaan Complex, Plot No. 3, B-2, Vasant Kunj, New Delhi 110 070
Phone: 91-11-4176-1620 • *Fax:* 91-11-4176-1630
www.hayhouse.co.in

———

Access New Knowledge.
Anytime. Anywhere.

Learn and evolve at your own pace
with the world's leading experts.

www.hayhouseU.com